By My Side
A Teen Prayer Companion

Victoria Shepp

saint mary's press

The publishing team included Gloria Shahin, editorial director; Steven Ellair, development editor; Joanna Dailey and Lorraine Kilmartin, contributing editors. Prepress and manufacturing coordinated by the production departments of Saint Mary's Press.

Cover image: © www.shutterstock.com

Printed in the United States of America

5037

ISBN 978-1-59982-171-9, Print
ISBN 978-1-59982-272-3, Digital

Introduction

By My Side: A Teen Prayer Companion was designed to provide you with an opportunity to be nourished, inspired, and challenged by Scripture. As people of faith, we are called to use Scripture for guidance and growth. The hope is that this resource will help you do this in a way that brings meaning and insight to the experiences of your life.

This resource can be used in a variety of ways. You can start any time in the year and follow the reflections day by day, or you can use the index in the back to focus your reflection on specific topics or issues that may be of particular interest to you.

If you like to write, keeping a journal can be a good companion to this resource. If you like to read, you can delve into the Bible more deeply by exploring larger portions of the Scripture identified each day. If you like music, let some quiet, reflective melodies or your favorite songs from church or youth ministry accompany you as you read. And if you are hurried and have little time, drop this resource in your backpack, keep it on your nightstand, or find a place where you might be able to access it for a quick reflection at the most convenient time. Regardless of how you approach it, the amount of time you have, or your knowledge of Scripture, this resource will help you begin a yearlong journey of growing in faith.

Acknowledgments

I'd like to express my appreciation to all who made this book possible. First, I would like to extend a great deal of thanks to all the staff at Saint Mary's Press for working with me to produce this book. Second, I would like to thank all the young people I've been blessed to journey with throughout my years as a companion of faith. Last and most important, I would like to thank my biological family and my faith family for their support; without it I would not have been able to start, let alone finish, this project. Special thanks to Steven Ellair and Paulette Smith, two special members of my faith family and former colleagues at the Archdiocese of Los Angeles, who were integral to this project.

New Year, Same You?

> For we know that if the earthly tent we live in is
> destroyed, we have a building from God, a house
> not made with hands, eternal in the heavens.
>
> (2 Corinthians 5:1)

This may seem like a heavy verse to begin a new year, but it helps us to remember that it is not the outer body that matters, but the inner self. It's common to make New Year's resolutions to eat less or to change the way we look or act. Maybe this is the year to start looking inward at our relationship with God. As we evaluate the previous year and start planning for a brand new one, we can take the time to focus on our relationship with God and with our faith community. We can ask ourselves, as we set our New Year goals: What is my relationship with God? How often am I spending time in prayer and reflection?

God, help me to turn my attention to our relationship in this new year, making it strong and faith-filled.

Confidence from Christ

> Do not, therefore, abandon that confidence of
> yours; it brings a great reward.
>
> (Hebrews 10:35)

If we have confidence in Christ, we are able to have confidence in ourselves. The unknown author who wrote to the Hebrews in the first century after Jesus' death encouraged those early believers to remain confident in Christ. This confidence, which we too can enjoy as Christians, has its rewards: a community of faith to journey with, a loving God to turn to, and the assurance that we can stand tall as followers of Christ. Do you put your confidence in Christ and his gifts? Can you draw on that confidence to develop your own self-esteem?

Christ, in whom I put my confidence, help me to find confidence in myself.

Accepting Others

> Just then his disciples came. They were astonished
> that he was speaking with a woman, but no one
> said, "What do you want?" or, "Why are you
> speaking with her?"

(John 4:27)

We may expect our friends to stay within our own group.
We might even ask, "Why are you speaking with her?"
if a friend talks to someone outside our circle. Jesus'
followers might have had that question when they saw
him sitting with a woman—a woman who was outcast by
her society. But they knew better than to ask. Jesus had let
them know that he needed to share himself with others,
even outsiders like this woman he met at the well. We too
need to be willing to share ourselves with outsiders. And if
we ever feel like an outsider ourselves, we can know that
Jesus sits and shares himself with us just as he did with the
woman at the well.

*Christ who sits with all, help me to be accepting of
others and to know that no matter what you accept
me.*

What's a Friend to Do?

> One who forgives an affront fosters friendship,
>   but one who dwells on disputes will alienate
>   a friend.

(Proverbs 17:9)

An affront can be an insult, a disrespectful action, or something that causes injury. Unfortunately our friends sometimes do hurt us in these ways. It is only human to want to retaliate, but the writer of Proverbs advises us to forgive. The writer knows that if we do not forgive, if we dwell on the affront, we alienate that friend. Although we may struggle to forgive serious injuries, many of the things that make us mad are minor. Is there someone you need to forgive in order to foster a friendship? If so, how can you express forgiveness? Do you need to ask for forgiveness? In either case, fostering a friendship is worth the effort.

Christ, my friend, forgive me if I have insulted you, and help me to foster friendship by forgiving others and asking for forgiveness as I need it.

Go against the Flow

> Do not be conformed to this world, but be transformed by the renewing of your minds, so that you may discern what is the will of God—what is good and acceptable and perfect.

> (Romans 12:2)

Sometimes others try to persuade us to do or say something that does not reflect our true and best self. Sometimes we respond to this pressure by acting like one of the crowd yet wondering if we really should be succumbing to pressure this way. At those times, we can recall Paul's words to the Romans and ask ourselves: Am I just conforming to the standard of my peers? Is this action "good and acceptable and perfect"? These questions can help us to discern the will of God.

God, my guide, help me to learn to discern what is good and acceptable and perfect, and to strive to do these things.

How Would I Treat Christ?

But when you thus sin against members of your family, and wound their conscience when it is weak, you sin against Christ.

(1 Corinthians 8:12)

When Paul wrote to the people of Corinth, he was helping them learn how to be followers of Christ, living in community. He knew it was hard not to fall into temptation or to tempt others. He also gave instructions on family life. He tells the Corinthians that if they sin against others or cause others to sin, they are sinning against Christ. When we regularly spend time with people, we can easily fall into bad behaviors: we can be mean to family members, lead them into a fight, or be disrespectful. Before we do something that might fall into those categories, we can ask ourselves, Is this the way I would treat Christ? Our answer can lead us to take the right action.

Christ, my brother, help me to treat my whole family with the same love I have for you.

Keeping Our Way Pure

How can young people keep their way pure?
By guarding it according to your word.

(Psalm 119:9)

When we are tempted, we may not remember what we can do to reduce the temptation. However, this psalm verse gives us a way to resist the temptation of impure actions. When we are faced with temptation, we might find help in remembering the psalmist's advice and guarding our actions according to God's Word. We can learn a phrase or two from Scripture to recall in a moment of temptation—or better yet, before that moment arrives. Listening to God's Word and repeating a memorized verse to ourselves may keep us from temptation and guard our way through life.

Dear God, help me to keep my way pure and to ensure that my actions are always according to your Word.

Cyberbullying in Scripture?

> Do to others as you would have them do to you.
>
> (Luke 6:31)

Although Jesus never witnessed cyberbullying, he knew that people did not always treat one another well. He gave us clear instructions about how to treat one another. There is no way around it: bullying is wrong. Although we may not be the one doing the bullying or the one being bullied, we do have a responsibility to speak out against it, report it, and be sure it is stopped. If we truly want to "do unto others," that means we never bully, and we never encourage bullying. It also means we do something about it because we'd want someone else to do that for us.

Compassionate Lord, help me to have compassion for those around me and to be a voice for those who need help.

Lions and Tigers and Tests

Save me from the mouth of the lion!
From the horns of the wild oxen you have
rescued me.

(Psalm 22:21)

Most of us do not have lions or wild oxen to worry about. But we do have the perils of modern life, which may sometimes seem just as daunting. As we face those things that scare us, we join others in a long tradition of calling on God. People of faith, like the psalmist, have always asked God to intervene. We can prepare for stressful challenges like studying for tests. We can make smart choices to help us stay safe, like wearing seat belts, choosing not to smoke, and making friends with people who do the same. Still, when faced with something scary, it is nice to know that our cry for help will be heard.

To you, my God, I lift my voice and know that you will be there to hear me.

Turning My Cheek

> But I say to you, Do not resist an evildoer. But if anyone strikes you on the right cheek, turn the other also. . . .
>
> (Matthew 5:39)

When we hear the instruction to turn the other cheek, we start to understand why some people thought Jesus was a radical. In Jesus' time it was common to think of "an eye for an eye" as a response to wrongdoing, so his teachings were as radical then as they are today. So what can we do about violence when we encounter it? We can indeed turn the other cheek and not hit back when hit, but we can also be the ones, like Jesus, who build the path for peace. Do you lash out in words or actions when others harm you? Do you hit your brother or sister when you fight? Do you play too rough on the ball field? Being a person of peace may be a little more difficult than it first sounds.

Gentle God of peace, help me to be peaceful in my thoughts and actions.

Living Faith

> For the law of the Spirit of life in Christ Jesus has
> set you free from the law of sin and of death.
>
> (Romans 8:2)

Most of us know the difference between right and wrong. We have received clear teachings from parents, teachers, and the Church. Complex issues may present gray areas, but most of our daily moral decisions are black and white. Even though our values are shaped by our faith, our family, and our community, we still make bad choices and do the wrong thing at times. But if our faith points us to our values, our faith can also help us to live them out. We are filled with grace when we experience God's forgiveness through the Sacraments. And we are blessed to be able to turn to the Word of God, which assures us that when we focus on living our life with the guidance of the Spirit, we really are set free from the law of sin.

Living God, be with me as I make decisions, and help me to live my faith and values in the law of the Spirit.

Feeling Lovesick?

> I adjure you, O daughters of Jerusalem,
>   by the gazelles or the wild does:
> do not stir up or awaken love
>   until it is ready!
>
> (Song of Solomon 2:7)

When we have a crush on someone, we want to rush into love, awaken it, and stir it up. Rushing love places pressure on us and on the object of our affection. When we think constantly about another person, we can lose ourselves. We might make poor decisions just to enjoy that feeling of being in love. Before rushing into love, it can be helpful to ask ourselves: Am I only in love with the idea of love? Do I know what I'm getting myself into? Do I know that this person will respect me? Listening to the answers to these questions can help to slow us down and allow love to come when it is ready.

God, who loves me forever, teach me to love tenderly and to not rush into anything. May I wait until love is ready for me and I am ready for it.

Doubts?

> Jesus said to him, "Have you believed because you have seen me? Blessed are those who have not seen and yet have come to believe."
>
> (John 20:29)

We Christians are asked to do something rather difficult: believe in something we cannot see. Thomas is often referred to as the original "doubter"; after the Resurrection, he needed to put his hands in Jesus' wounds in order to believe. Jesus says that we are blessed because we believe without seeing, but how can we believe in what we do not see? When we find ourselves doubting, we can remember what Jesus told Thomas about those who believe without seeing, and let ourselves be blessed.

Jesus, who helped Thomas to believe, help me to believe. May I tell others about you, the most powerful force in my life.

What Do You Value?

> To whom will you liken me and make me equal,
> and compare me, as though we were alike?
>
> (Isaiah 46:5)

As Christians we say that God is important. But what else do we value? We may place more value on our electronics and technology than on God; we may place more value on sports or a movie star; we may place more value on things, forgetting that the one who made us is the one with the highest value. Are you putting things above God? Are you spending too much time or money on things in comparison to the amount of time you spend in prayer, praise, and serving God? If the answer to these questions is yes, it's time to turn the tables on what you value.

You, my God, are more precious than anything else. Help me to remember to place you higher than all of my things.

Applying Ourselves

> If you are willing, my child, you can be disciplined,
> and if you apply yourself you will become
> clever.
>
> (Sirach 6:32)

Not everyone can get straight A's, be at the top of the class, or excel in every subject. But we all can and should do our best. The wise words of Sirach remind us of a simple strategy: applying ourselves. We do not need to rank first in all that we do, but as a way to honor God we should be doing our best. Having discipline and applying ourselves does not guarantee straight A's, but Sirach assures us that we will become clever. As we plan our time, we can ask ourselves: Am I taking time to study? Am I doing my best? What am I learning that will help me in the future?

God of wisdom, help me to be disciplined in my studies so that I may be wise in your ways.

Put Away Anger

> Put away from you all bitterness and wrath and
> anger and wrangling and slander, together
> with all malice, and be kind to one another,
> tenderhearted, forgiving one another, as God in
> Christ has forgiven you.
>
> (Ephesians 4:31–32)

As members of a Christian community, we are called to love one another. Although we may become angry at times, we need to try to put anger aside and strive to be kind. This can be difficult to do, especially in a family or community. When we are close to people, it is easy to get angry. But closeness also allows us to be tenderhearted and forgiving. Putting away anger requires us to ask questions like: Am I holding on to anger that I should let go of? Can I put this aside and concentrate on the good in the person or situation?

Lord, make me to be like you, slow to anger and quick to forgive.

Promises, Promises

> I have set my bow in the clouds, and it shall be a
> sign of the covenant between me and the earth.
>
> (Genesis 9:13)

We make promises all the time: promises to clean our
rooms, call a friend, or help a sibling. We rarely make
promises we do not intend to keep. God provided a
sign of the covenant he made at the time of Noah. The
rainbow was a sign that God would never again flood
the earth to destroy it. Signs help make our promises real.
For Boy Scouts and Girl Scouts, a hand sign represents the
Scout Promise. When we pass our drivers' test, our license
is a sign of our commitment to obey the traffic laws. What
if we had a sign for all of our promises? The next time we
make a promise, we might consider creating some sort of
sign that helps to make it real.

*God, you've kept your promises to your people; help
me to keep my promises, and inspire me to remember
the importance of the commitments I make.*

Christ Can Calm Us

He woke up and rebuked the wind, and said to the sea, "Peace! Be still!" Then the wind ceased, and there was a dead calm.

(Mark 4:39)

Christ has the power to calm a stormy sea, yet we sometimes forget to call on him when we are in far less serious situations. The disciples called on him, and he took care of them. He does that for us too when we call on him. Sometimes we get so caught up in an issue or problem that we forget to call on God. When we find ourselves getting overly stressed or concerned about something, it helps to ask, Can I call on God to help me here? We know that the answer is yes. Calling on the calming power of the Risen Christ can be calming in itself. Calling on him will provide even more calm, as the disciples in the boat found out on that stormy night.

Christ, who calms the sea, be near me when I cry out to you in times of stress.

Followers Then and Now

> They devoted themselves to the apostles' teaching and fellowship, to the breaking of bread and the prayers.
>
> (Acts of the Apostles 2:42)

When we think about what it means to be Christian, we might think of wearing a cross or crucifix, or blessing ourselves with holy water as we enter a church. These are things we do to show we are Christian, but we also must act as Christians. The earliest followers of Christ, as recorded in Acts, were given some clear instructions. Do you devote time to learning about your faith and the Bible? Do you spend time with other Christians sharing faith? Do you participate in the celebration of the Eucharist and actively pray with the community? Do you pray on your own? These key elements of the Christian life were essential to the first followers of Christ and are essential for us today.

Risen Lord, help me to always show my Christian identity through my actions.

Grand Forgiveness

> Then Jesus said, "Father, forgive them; for they do
> not know what they are doing."
>
> (Luke 23:34)

We are often challenged to forgive others. When
someone's actions or words offend us, we may want
to be angry rather than offer the offender forgiveness.
When we feel hurt, it is hard to forgive. Jesus gives us
the ultimate example of forgiveness during his Passion.
As he was being crucified, he forgave his executioners.
How can we learn from this example and find strength to
forgive those who offend us? As we feel our injury, and
experience betrayal, we can answer these questions: Am
I going to let this action or experience separate me from
the God who forgives? Can I be like Christ and forgive
this person?

*Christ my Savior, you died on the cross for us and
showed us what forgiveness means. I thank you and
praise you, and I seek your guidance in becoming a
person of forgiveness like you.*

Washing Feet

> "So if I, your Lord and Teacher, have washed your feet, you also ought to wash one another's feet."
>
> (John 13:14)

Jesus gives us many examples of service. He healed the sick, made the blind see, and restored dignity to outcasts. We learn that we too are called to be people of service in his example of washing the disciples' feet. Performing the task of a servant, Jesus sets his followers on the path of service. Many people serve us, and many provide inspiring examples of serving others. When do you serve out of love? How can you follow Jesus' example of humble service? Who in your community needs your service so that they too may follow Jesus?

Although I may never wash anyone's feet, I thank you, Christ, for reminding me to do as you did and to serve others humbly.

Happy Company

> Happy are those who make
>   the Lord their trust,
> who do not turn to the proud,
>   to those who go astray after false gods.
>
>   (Psalm 40:4)

God created us to be social, and when we choose our group of friends, we have multiple options. We can choose a group that supports a healthy, holy lifestyle, or we can choose a group that does not. If we choose people who "go astray after false gods" like material objects, premarital sex, or illegal substances, we will find ourselves surrounded by those who experience what they think is happiness, but discover that it is fleeting and mostly false. When choosing companions, it is helpful to ask ourselves: Are these the type of people who know and walk with God? Or will they go after the false gods who lead me away from true happiness in God?

God in whom I place my trust, I turn to you and ask that you inspire me to choose friends who walk with you.

Wishing or Hoping

> . . . and hope does not disappoint us, because
> God's love has been poured into our hearts
> through the Holy Spirit that has been given to us.
>
> (Romans 5:5)

We might wish we were taller, wish we would win the lottery, or wish the superintendent would cancel school, but we know such wishes are a little fanciful. When we have hope that is rooted in our faith, however, we know it will not fail us. We can draw on hope because of God's love for us. We who hope in God do so with the knowledge that God provides what we need. Most important, we hope in Christ's Resurrection, and we know that this hope will not disappoint us. So when we use the word *hope*, let's be sure we are not confusing it with *wish*.

Christ, who is risen from the dead, help me to focus on a hope rooted in God's love for me, rather than on my fanciful wishes.

Big Love

> For God so loved the world that he gave his only
> Son, so that everyone who believes in him may
> not perish but may have eternal life.
>
> (John 3:16)

We may think we see true love when we see that couple at school always attached at the hip or when we watch a romantic movie. But true love is much more than romance and googly eyes. True love is godly. None of us will likely have to sacrifice the way Jesus did when he died on the cross, but we will have to make sacrifices for love. We might know of parents who have sacrificed to give their child a particular opportunity, or of a teacher who has sacrificed time for her students. When we find ourselves thinking about love, we can ask: Is this a godly love? Am I willing to make sacrifices for this love?

God of sacrificial love, help me to keep your ultimate act of love as the inspiration for how I love others.

Drawing on Hope

> You said, "Woe is me! The Lord has added
> sorrow to my pain; I am weary with my groaning,
> and I find no rest."
>
> (Jeremiah 45:3)

We sometimes feel like we're being hit while we're down. We might feel that God is not listening or is not even near. We understand the words of Jeremiah, who does not see or feel God's presence. Although we feel as if no one is listening or caring, we can rest assured that there is hope. This hope becomes important in moments of pain. By drawing on that hope, we become like Jeremiah, who was later able to move through pain and suffering. Like Jeremiah we can find light at the end and see that God was indeed with us through it all.

God who knows my deepest suffering, gently remind me of your presence and show me your light.

Accepting All

> There is neither Jew nor Greek, there is no longer
> slave or free, there is no longer male and female;
> for all of you are one in Christ Jesus.
>
> (Galatians 3:28)

If we rewrote this passage for today's young people, how would it sound? This rewording might help us to imagine what being accepted by all and accepting all would look like in our daily life. But wanting to be accepted can sometimes get in the way of accepting others. Are there any people that you don't accept? What are the reasons you are not accepting them? Do you really want to act this way, or are you doing it to be accepted by others? By answering such questions, we can see what our motivation is and remind ourselves that just as we want acceptance, so do others. If we strive to accept others, we may find acceptance for who we truly are.

God of love, who accepts me just as I am, help me to be accepting of others, and let my motivation be guided by your ways.

Creator God

> God saw everything that he had made, and
> indeed, it was very good. And there was evening
> and there was morning, the sixth day.
>
> (Genesis 1:31)

We know God likes the results of his creative work. God said after each day that the new creation was good. We can look around at the earth and sky, animals and plants, planets and stars and know that they are good. What about when we look in the mirror or look at another person? Do we know that what we see is good too? If we take the words of Genesis to heart, we must definitely believe that we are good too. Our essential goodness is sometimes hidden deep within, but we know that God loves all of his creations. God loves the earth and sea and sky. God loves the animals and plants and all the critters. And God most certainly loves us and knows we are very good.

Creator God, help me to remember my goodness and the goodness of others.

Moses Is Called

> When the Lord saw that he had turned aside to
> see, God called to him out of the bush, "Moses,
> Moses! And he said, "Here I am."
>
> (Exodus 3:4)

We might think Moses is lucky because God so clearly
called him. God does not seem to use burning bushes to
call followers today. However, God does call each of us.
God has given each of us a purpose, just like Moses.
Perhaps God does give us our own version of a burning
bush, but we may walk by it if we do not take time to
listen for him. We need to pay attention to know what
God is calling us to do. One way to begin to develop
attentiveness is to practice just listening, sitting in quiet.
Instead of asking questions, we can take some time this
day to be still and listen

Here I am, Lord, listening for your call.

Jesus' Mission Is Ours

"The Spirit of the Lord is upon me,
    because he has anointed me
        to bring good news to the poor.
He has sent me to proclaim release to the captives
    and recovery of sight to the blind,
        to let the oppressed go free,
to proclaim the year of the Lord's favor."

(Luke 4:18–19)

Jesus announces his mission in a way that inspires us to follow his example. When we look around, we see physically poor people who have no food and shelter, and spiritually poor people who have no faith. We see captives of abuse, self-hatred, and addiction. We know that there are visually blind people and others who refuse to see the beauty of life. The oppressed may be modern-day slaves or victims of bullying. Whatever we see, when we hear Jesus' mission we must ask ourselves: What am I doing to help others? How can I be like Jesus right here and right now?

Jesus, my brother, may I follow your lead and help others in need.

Creation Needs Us

Praise the Lord! . . .
Mountains and all hills,
    fruit trees and all cedars!
Wild animals and all cattle,
    creeping things and flying birds!

(Psalm 148:1,9–10)

Animals, plants, earth, and sky would praise God if they could speak. However, would all of creation praise us humans? We do not always treat creation with the love and care it deserves. The earth and all its inhabitants—animal and plant—are part of God's creation, and we are called to be caretakers, good stewards. Unfortunately we sometimes act as if the earth and its inhabitants exist just for us to use and abuse. Are you a good steward of God's creation? Are you doing your part to care for God's creation so future generations will benefit from your actions?

God of all creation, help me to be a good steward, and may those who step on earth benefit from my actions.

I Am Wonderfully Made

For it was you who formed my inward parts;
  you knit me together in my mother's womb.
I praise you, for I am fearfully and wonderfully
    made.
  Wonderful are your works;
that I know very well.

(Psalm 139:13–14)

If we really believed that God made us wonderfully, we would not worry about who we are. When we look in the mirror and see our faults, when we fail to make a team, or when we struggle with a certain subject, it is easy to forget the psalmist's words. God does make us wonderfully, although it may take time to figure out who God intends us to be. Are you trying to be the person *you* want to be or the person God means for you to be? As that answer begins to reveal itself to us, we are able to become who we truly are, the person God intends us to be.

God who created me, may I become aware of just how wonderfully you made me; may I learn to live as the wonderful person you intend me to be.

Facing Authority

"When you stand before him, have no fear in your heart, but tell him what you have just said, and he will treat you well."

(Judith 10:16)

During an armed conflict, the enemy commander's guards advised Judith to face their leader with self-assurance. We can have that same assurance when we need to face someone in authority. We can talk to the principal of our school, a civic leader, or a potential boss with confidence if we can prepare ahead of time. We can review the purpose of the meeting, plan what we will say, and consider how to show respect. If we properly prepare for an encounter, we boost our self-esteem. The next time we have an appointment with an authority figure, we can ask ourselves: Am I standing tall because I am prepared and respectful? Does my self-esteem show in my interactions?

Lord, help me to grow in confidence and self-esteem so that I may respectfully face and interact with authority figures.

No Hostility

> For he is our peace; in his flesh he has made both groups into one and has broken down the dividing wall, that is, the hostility between us.
>
> (Ephesians 2:14)

Accepting others means we have to break down dividing walls, just as the early Christians, Jews, and Gentiles did. We have to rely on the love of God to help us be one and to remove the barriers that get in the way of unity. Sometimes we create these barriers. Sometimes others create them. Regardless of the source, removing the hostility is essential to creating peace. If we look at those we have not accepted and ask ourselves, Can I do something to break down the barrier standing between me and that person or group? we can come closer to knowing what barrier stands in the way of acceptance.

Lord, who loves all equally, help me to remove the barriers that are keeping me from fully accepting others.

A Real Friend

> And there are friends who sit at your table, but
> they will not stand by you in time of trouble.
>
> (Sirach 6:10)

We sit with a group of friends during lunch. These friends
may or may not be the same friends that will be at our side
when we really need them. Likewise we may be willing to
have fun with friends, but if we have to choose between
helping them and doing something fun, what happens?
If we want to have good friends, we need to *be* good
friends. We also need to choose friends carefully. Having
many friends is not as important as having true friends.
Before calling someone a friend, we can ask ourselves:
Am I willing to give up something fun to help this person?
Do I think this person would be willing to do that for me?

*Holy Spirit, inspire me to be the type of friend who is
willing to stand by the side of my friends, and inspire
me to choose friends who would do the same for me.*

Walking with the Wise

> Whoever walks with the wise becomes wise, but
> the companion of fools suffers harm.
>
> (Proverbs 13:20)

Choosing which group to walk with can be tricky. We
may think that by walking with the "cool kids," we will
automatically be cool; we may base our choice of friends
solely on image. The writer of Proverbs reminds us that
our choice should not be about who is "cool" or not, but
that we are best served by choosing to walk with those
who have wisdom. Are you walking with certain people
because of their image, or because you will become a
better, wiser person by being friends with them?

*God of all wisdom, I desire to learn your ways and
to become wiser and closer to you. Help me choose
to walk with the wise rather than be a companion to
the foolish.*

Honoring Parents

Honor your father and your mother, so that your days may be long in the land that the Lord your God is giving you.

(Exodus 20:12)

We know we should honor our parents. We have learned the Ten Commandments, and we know that they call us to honor our parents. Yet we often find ourselves ignoring our parents at best and outright dishonoring them at worst. This commandment reminds us to evaluate our relationship with our parents. Thinking about how we treat them can also help us to identify issues we need to talk to them about. For example, we might ask: Why do I get mad at my mom when she asks me about homework? Is it because I feel guilty that I have not done it well? Is it because I feel she distrusts me? If we can learn to have good conversations with our parents, we will be much more likely to honor them.

God, my most loving parent, help me to honor my parents and know that as I do this, I honor you.

Faithful to Abstaining

The Lord loves those who hate evil;
　　he guards the lives of the faithful;
　　he rescues them from the hand of the wicked.

(Psalm 97:10)

Our Church teaches us to abstain from sexual activity until we are married. Although we should not judge or wish punishment on others, we can be certain that there are rewards for being faithful. The psalmist assures us that God guards those who are faithful to his ways. God will help us if someone is tempting or pressuring us to participate in sexual activity. That person may not be wicked, but her or his actions might be leading us to sin. So calling on God in times of sexual temptation and pressure may help.

God, I know you want me to abstain from sexual activity. Give me strength to continue to resist temptation.

Group Bullying

> From then on Pilate tried to release him, but the
> Jews cried out, "If you release this man, you are
> no friend of the emperor. Everyone who claims to
> be a king sets himself against the emperor."
>
> (John 19:12)

Sometimes it is easy to get caught up in making fun of someone or in making someone feel like an outsider. We are more like Pilate than we may want to admit when we participate in this kind of bullying. Like Pilate, we may allow the crowd to persuade us, or even incite us. Going along with a mean-spirited crowd is just as hurtful as being mean all on our own. When the crowd is laughing, we can make sure we are not taking part in bullying by asking ourselves the simple question, How would I feel if everyone was laughing at me?

Lord of compassion, help me to be aware of my actions when I am in a group.

God Is Near

Do not fear, for I am with you.

(Isaiah 43:5)

We all experience fear. Some of us fear dogs or spiders, or we may fear speaking out in class, or fear losing someone close to us. Some fears can keep us safe, like the fear of being hit by a car when we cross the street, but other fears can prevent us from growing and developing into the person God calls us to be. We can listen to our healthy fears, and we can also trust God when we feel afraid of things we cannot control. God wants us to know that when we experience fear we are not alone. The next time we are afraid for a big or small reason, we can remember Isaiah's words and know that God is indeed near.

God, who comforts me, help me to remember that you are near during those times I feel afraid.

Violence-Free

A violent tempered person will pay the penalty.

(Proverbs 19:19)

Most of us have learned from an early age that we need to use words instead of our fists when expressing anger. If we see violence, we need to report it. If we get so mad we want to be violent, we need to step away, and maybe even seek help. Not only will violence get us in trouble, it is against God's Law. When we are caught up in anger and feel it growing, it can be helpful to ask ourselves: Why am I so mad? What other action can I take? Who can I talk with about this situation? Answering those questions can help us to slow our anger and deal with it in a more productive way.

God of peace, help me to walk in peace and to help others do so as well.

Shared Values

> Finally, all of you, have unity of spirit, sympathy, love for one another, a tender heart, and a humble mind.
>
> (1 Peter 3:8)

We hear a lot of talk about values. School communities may talk about common values, politicians talk about American values, and our families base decisions and rules on their own set of values. Our Church teaches us the values we share as Christians. Working together to live out and develop these shared values builds community. We each need to find groups of people who help us live as faith-filled Christians. When we find these groups and surround ourselves with people who share the same values, we can strengthen the values that are so important to us and that bind us together as a community of faith.

Father, Son, and Holy Spirit, Three in One, help me to find others that walk in your ways as I try to bring my Christian values and faith to life.

Dating and Faith

> Therefore a man leaves his father and his mother
> and clings to his wife, and they become one flesh.
>
> (Genesis 2:24)

God provides a way for couples to become one. Beautiful things come from great relationships, and we likely want to experience all those things for ourselves. We need to remember that marriage, becoming one, is a sacramental privilege. Dating is a way to discover what kind of person we want to enter into this Sacrament with. If we consider dating as part of how we live our faith, then we can anticipate and look forward to becoming one with another, but we don't need to rush it. We can use dating to find someone who supports and encourages our faith. Dating may test our faith at times, but dating can reinforce our faith as well.

God, I look forward to knowing what or whom you have in store for me.

Seeing Faith

> Now faith is the assurance of things hoped for, the conviction of things not seen.
>
> (Hebrews 11:1)

We modern people are not much different from our ancestors in faith. We have a desire to touch and see proof of things before believing in them. Our ancestors in faith also wanted proof. They, like us, had to rely on believing in what they hoped for and maintain the conviction of things not seen. As the wind blows, we have evidence that air surrounds us. As God moves in us and throughout the world, we believe in his presence with more and more assurance. What things do you believe in that you cannot see? Can you apply that same faith to your belief in God?

God, who shows us the unseen, help me to have faith in you and your ways.

Sell It All?

> Jesus, looking at him, loved him and said, "You lack one thing: go, sell what you own, and give the money to the poor, and you will have treasure in heaven; then come, follow me."
>
> (Mark 10:21)

Jesus does not want us to be poor, but he does want us to know that money is not important for salvation. Faith and generosity are more important than wealth and prestige. Getting into the Kingdom of Heaven is more important than getting into high-end restaurants or stores. By asking ourselves how we spend our money, and by keeping our focus on Jesus' teachings, we stay on track with the requirements of our faith. No matter what our circumstances, we will do well to follow Jesus' instructions and use our gifts to help those who are poor.

Generous God, help me to focus more on you than on riches; may I be generous to others in whatever way I am able.

Saint Valentine's Day

> Love is patient; love is kind: love is not envious or
> boastful or arrogant or rude.

> (1 Corinthians 13:4–5)

Even if we do not have a special someone in our life
this Valentine's Day, we can still take today to practice
patience, kindness, openness, humility, and courtesy. As
we are surrounded by modern signs of love, such as hearts
and flowers, chocolate and kisses, we might think that
love is the same as romance. But Paul's signs of love will
stand the test of time. Today we can challenge ourselves
to be patient toward someone, to be kind, to compliment
someone sincerely, to be humble, and to be polite. When
we choose to treat people in this way, we will experience
what the spirit of love really feels like.

God of love, teach me to love as you do, patiently,
kindly, and without envy or arrogance.

Planning

> Commit your work to the Lord,
>   and your plans will be established.
>
>   (Proverbs 16:3)

When we want to succeed in school, in sports, in music, or in other endeavors, we may experience pressure. If we see how these daily events and activities fit into God's desire for us and take time to plan, we benefit with less stress and better results. Because we place such high expectations on ourselves at times, good planning skills can help us to meet those expectations. As we work toward our goals, we can ask ourselves: Is this a plan that the Lord will smile on? Will it help me in my relationship with God? with others? Will it bring me closer to my goals?

Lord of good work, I make this prayer in your name. May I set realistic expectations for myself, plan well, and keep on your path.

Slow to Anger

> You must understand this, my beloved: let
> everyone be quick to listen, slow to speak, slow
> to anger; for your anger does not produce God's
> righteousness.

> (James 1:19–20)

We all know people with short fuses. They are quick to anger, they do not listen well, and they fly off the handle with angry words or even violent actions. Sometimes we call them "hotheads." The author of this New Testament letter advises us to have long fuses or fuses that do not light at all. It can be helpful to ask ourselves questions like these: Am I really listening, or am I busy coming up with my own reply? Can I slow my anger down to hear what this person is saying, and think before I respond? If we can slow ourselves down, either by thinking about these questions or by simply counting to ten, we will be able to more easily follow the instructions we find in this Scripture verse.

I am thankful that you, gentle God, are slow to anger and quick to listen. Help me to be more like you and less like a hothead.

Promises Made

> If you will only obey the Lord your God . . . the
> Lord your God will set you high above all the
> nations of the earth; all these blessings shall come
> upon you and overtake you, if you obey the Lord
> your God.
>
> (Deuteronomy 28:1)

When we keep our commitments to God, we can expect positive outcomes. God follows through on his promise to bless us, and the result is a win-win situation. If we can carry this type of win-win thinking into all of our commitments with others, we may receive the same positive outcomes. Making agreements and keeping them can be two very different things. Have you ever let others down by not following through?

May I keep my commitments just as you keep yours, God of promise and blessing.

Protect Me, O God

Deliver me from my enemies, O my God;
protect me from those who rise up against
me.

(Psalm 59:1)

We know that there are safe places like storm shelters, hurricane routes, and well-designed buildings that can withstand earthquakes. And we know that there are safe places where we can be ourselves, such as a counselor's office, a grandparent's living room, or our best friend's house. God also gives us a safe place where we can go, no matter where we may be physically. This safe place can be found in moments of prayer when we turn to God and ask for protection, strength, and love.

O Holy Protector, shelter me from things and people that are trying to harm me. Be my safe harbor in times of trouble.

Choices

> Because he himself was tested by what he suffered, he is able to help those who are being tested.
>
> (Hebrews 2:18)

When we are young, temptation may come in the form of the cookie jar or our sister's unlocked diary. As we get older, many more temptations face us. Life becomes more complex as temptations become more significant. Developing a way to manage temptations is a life skill that will help now and in the future. When making a decision about right and wrong, we can ask ourselves questions like these: If I make this choice, can I tell my parents about it without making up a story? Would I make this choice if my grandmother was watching? In some cases, those questions are easy to answer. If we begin by practicing on minor or easy decisions, making the right choice with more serious temptations may become easier.

Good and gracious God, I turn to you in times of temptation. May your grace and strength aid me as I make tough choices.

Forgiving Family

> "So have no fear; I myself will provide for you and your little ones." In this way [Joseph] reassured them, speaking kindly to them.

> (Genesis 50:21)

Siblings can make us feel weak, small, insignificant, or unintelligent. If we have older siblings, we might strive to keep up with them. If we have younger siblings, we might make them feel inadequate or unwelcome. The story of Joseph and his brothers reminds us of the deep bonds that siblings have with one another. Even after they had treated him so poorly, Joseph forgives his brothers and even takes care of them when he is an adult. As we reflect on our own relationship with siblings, we can ask: Have I treated my siblings fairly? Have they done something I need to forgive?

Protect my siblings, and make me a good example, friend, and companion to them. I make this prayer in the name of Jesus Christ, my brother.

To Do Justice

> He has told you, O mortal, what is good;
>   and what does the Lord require of you
> but to do justice, and to love kindness,
>   and to walk humbly with your God?
>
> (Micah 6:8)

When we clean up a beach or serve a meal in a shelter or write letters to end human trafficking, we are following in Jesus' footsteps of service. Often we think service includes only those things that directly help someone. Although service can be direct social service—like reading to children at a hospital—it can also be working toward social change—like calling for wider access to health care. Direct social service is called charity, and working toward social change is called justice. Both work together: through our charity work, we help individuals meet their basic needs, and through the work of justice, we help to correct long-term problems in communities.

As I walk humbly with you, Lord, help me to be a person of service and justice.

Peace and Happiness

> Keep on doing the things that you have learned
> and received and heard and seen in me, and the
> God of peace will be with you.

> (Philippians 4:9)

Some happy people have a secret that can benefit us. The secret is that they are filled with the peace of God. When we are filled with God's peace, we are able to experience happiness more fully. The writer of this New Testament letter urges the Philippians to remain faithful to the Gospel they have received. What is keeping you from knowing God's peace right now? Have you turned away from what you have learned and received from the Church? When we are faithful to the Gospel, we find the peace of God and our happiness grows.

God of peace and happiness, let me be with you in peace so I may be open to the happiness that flows from you.

Why Hope?

> The king came down to him and said, "This trouble is from the Lord! Why should I hope in the Lord any longer?"
>
> (2 Kings 6:33)

Do you ever feel as if some of your troubles come from God? As we try to become better followers of Christ, we may experience times when it seems like our lives are complicated by being Christian. It might even tempt us to lose faith or hope. Friends who do not understand our desire to live a Christian life may turn away from us, or a teacher or coach may penalize us if we miss a class, practice, or game because we choose to be involved in our church. This kind of response from some people can seem frustrating. But it is important to recall the hope that we have as Christians. By focusing on that hope, we will be able to see the blessings God has in store for us when we trust in him.

Lord of all hope, help me to stay focused on your ways, be a voice of your hope, and know that you will always be with me.

Only with Love

> If I speak in the tongues of mortals and of angels, but do not have love, I am a noisy gong or a clanging cymbal.
>
> (1 Corinthians 13:1)

Imagine a singer on stage in front of thousands of fans. As she opens her mouth to sing her hit song, a noisy, meaningless gonging sound comes forth that makes the fans cover their ears. We are like that singer if we do not have love. If we try to do something good, like community service, just to get credit for it, and not out of love, our good deed is as meaningless as a noisy gong. Jesus Christ did everything out of love, and we are given his example to follow. Are you doing anything just because it might look good on a college or job application, or are you acting out of love? Reflecting on these questions will keep us from being a noisy gong.

May all my actions be done in love, and may you hear my voice, not a noisy gong, echoing in your Kingdom. I pray to you, Lord of all love.

Turn to Christ in Suffering

> He said to her, "Daughter, your faith has made you well; go in peace and be healed of your disease."
>
> (Mark 5:34)

Suffering takes many forms. We can suffer physical pain and we can suffer spiritual pain. We are not alone in our suffering, even when it seems as if we are. Jesus feels our pain and knows when we reach out to him for healing. When we turn to him, even if we are timid about it, he is ready to help us. For suffering caused by such things as abuse, bullying, depression, and disease, we can turn to God as well as to experts or trusted adults. We must ask for help when we need it—from both God and the people God provides for us.

Christ the healer, I know you feel my pain; help me to heal and to find those who can help me as I need it.

Let's Not Lose Ourselves

> What does it profit them if they gain the whole world, but lose or forfeit themselves?
>
> (Luke 9:25)

When those students who "rule" the school walk down the hall, they seem to have gained the whole world. We may want to be as popular as they seem to be. Although being popular is not bad, if we act like someone other than ourselves just to be popular, we could be doing just what Jesus warned about: losing ourselves. As we navigate our way around school or other communities, we need to ask ourselves: Am I being true to who I am? Or am I acting in a way that forfeits what I value: my relationship with my family, church community, or God? If our actions are appropriate and aligned with our values and we still become popular, then we will know it is for the right reasons.

I know you understand my desire for popularity, so guide me, Lord, to be the person I am meant to be rather than letting me forfeit myself.

The Shepherd

The Lord is my shepherd, I shall not want.

(Psalm 23:1)

We often hear of God as the shepherd, but many of us do not know what a shepherd does. As we define this term, we learn why this image is popular. Shepherds did more than lead the sheep; they protected them from wolves and thieves, and they kept watch over them and guarded them. For people of biblical times, sheep and shepherds were a common sight. People saw how well shepherds cared for their sheep and realized that the comparison between God and a shepherd was a good one. Who in our time cares for others like a shepherd? And how might that person demonstrate characteristics that God has? Perhaps we could write our own psalm-like poem, describing God in a new way.

Good Shepherd, protect, care for, and guide me today and all the days of my life.

Anointed for God

> Then Samuel took the horn of oil, and anointed
> him in the presence of his brothers; and the spirit
> of the Lord came mightily upon David from that
> day forward.

> (1 Samuel 16:13)

Sometimes someone sees something in us we do not see in ourselves. Maybe a teacher or coach points to us, through our peers, and says, "You!" This can be scary or exciting or both. We might not know why we're being chosen, but we know we are being called to do something out of the ordinary. God calls us in a similar way, and we may not know exactly what we're being called to do. In our Baptism and Confirmation, we are anointed with oil as David was, and, like him, we will learn what God is calling us to do. As we wait for this calling, we can be assured that the Holy Spirit will help us to see and respond to it at the right time.

Lord, help me to be ready to answer your call.

Consider the Poor

Happy are those who consider the poor;
the Lord delivers them in the day of trouble.

(Psalm 41:1)

"Considering" the poor does not seem too demanding until we look into the meaning of the word *consider*. The synonyms for *consider* include *think carefully about, pay attention to,* and *reflect on*. Thinking carefully about the poor means really looking at them, not just rushing by them. When we pay attention to them, the poor become more real to us, and we will be more likely to help them. Reflecting on the poor may cause us to be grateful for the things we have. As we walk in our cities or work in soup kitchens, it can be helpful to ask ourselves, What does this person, who seems to be poor, have to teach me? If we care for those who are poor and try to learn from them, we can be assured that the Lord will deliver us in our day of trouble.

Lord, help me to be more mindful of the poor. May I learn the lessons they can teach me.

All Things Are from Him

> All things came into being through him, and
> without him not one thing came into being.
>
> (John 1:3)

Because all things came into being through Christ, we
know that the created world is a gift that we must preserve
for future generations. Thanks to science, we know how
our lifestyle impacts the earth and its inhabitants. We know
that car exhaust can come back to the earth in the form
of polluted rain; pesticides can seep into the ground and
cause water to be undrinkable; throwing trash into storm
drains pollutes the ocean and damages sea life. Yet with
all that knowledge, many still continue to disregard the
teaching that everything comes into being through Christ.
Are you doing your part to protect God's gifts in nature?

*All things came into being through you, O Christ;
help me to honor and respect these things.*

Who Am I?

> He said to them, "But who do you say that I am?"
> Peter answered, "The Messiah of God."
>
> (Luke 9:20)

We don't often ask others to tell us who we are, but we do often look to others for approval of who we are. We may sometimes try to look like others, and we may sometimes try to act like others. But God wants us to be ourselves. Jesus asked others to tell him who they thought he was so they could share in the Good News of salvation. Jesus may ask us: Who do you say you are? How do you show others who you are? Are you being the person God wants you to be, or are you trying to be the person others want you to be? If we ask these questions about ourselves and answer honestly, we may be more able to become the person God calls us to be.

God, who wants me to be me, help me to know and accept myself more and more each day.

Loving Self

". . . You shall love your neighbor as yourself."

(Matthew 22:39)

Many times we hear the command to "love your neighbor" but don't hear the second part: "as yourself." However, in order to love our neighbors, we have to love ourselves. Many of us have a hard time with this. Some of us might not be able to identify those things that are good about ourselves. But if we want to take the command of Jesus seriously, we need to work on the "as yourself" part of his command of love. As we look at ourselves physically, spiritually, and personally, we can ask: What do I do well? What things do people tell me I am good at? When I receive a compliment, do I listen and thank the person, or brush it off?

God, you love me no matter what I accomplish or how I look. Help me to love myself so that I may follow your command to love others.

One Body

> Now you are the body of Christ and individually
> members of it.
>
> (1 Corinthians 12:27)

Just as the eye is part of something bigger, the body,
we are part of something bigger too. Paul explains this
concept to the Corinthians, and it has relevance for us
today. An eye isn't any good if it is taken out of the body.
In the same way, God does not intend us to exist apart
from others. When we embrace others, we function well.
As members of the Body of Christ, we must accept all
of the other parts of the Body who help to make up this
community. Because we are part of the Body of Christ, it
is helpful for us to ask ourselves: Do I accept all others into
this community of faith? Do I recognize the contribution
others make to the Body of Christ?

*Christ, my brother, help me to be a positive,
accepting, healthy member of your Body.*

Tough Times and True Friends

Since I am convinced of this, I know that I will remain and continue with all of you for your progress and joy in faith, so that I may share abundantly in your boasting in Christ Jesus when I come to you again.

(Philippians 1:25–26)

Paul wrote that he would remain loyal and true to his friends. We can show our loyalty to our friends in many ways. One way is when our friends go through tough times. If a friend is being bullied, we step in. When a friend is hurting, we try to help him or her or seek out someone who can. True friends don't abandon each other. A good way to make sure we're being true friends is to ask ourselves: Am I true to my friends when they really need me? Can they call me and count on me when times are tough?

Christ, who stays with us through everything, help me to be a true friend to others.

Choosing Support

> I urge you, brothers and sisters, to keep an eye
> on those who cause dissensions and offenses, in
> opposition to the teaching that you have learned;
> avoid them.
>
> (Romans 16:17)

We grow up hearing about peer pressure. Most parents have asked something like, "If all the kids were jumping off the bridge, would you do the same?" They want us to resist blindly going along with the crowd. But peer pressure can be a good thing too. When we choose peers who lead us, or even pressure us, in positive ways, peer pressure can actually be healthy. So in addition to avoiding negative peer pressure, we can develop a group of peers who want us to achieve and who encourage us to make good decisions. And we can do the same for them. When we encounter negative peer pressure, it is easier to make the right choices if others back us up.

Loving God, as I move in and among my peers, help me to choose friends who want me to be my best, friends that I can support as well.

God's Children

> He was the son . . . of Joseph . . . son of
> Enos, son of Seth, son of Adam, son of God.
>
> (Luke 3:23,38)

Genealogy is the study of one's family tree. The genealogy of Jesus in the Gospel of Luke shows his connection to all of humanity: he is a child of Adam and a child of God. We may know something about our own family tree. Some of us can trace our ancestors back to another country or to Native American communities. However, some us may not have the ability to trace our lineage because of slavery, loss of records, or adoption. Regardless of our family tree, we are all connected to others before us, and we are all children of God. What do you know about your family tree, and how does this affect your identity? What does it mean to you to be a child of God? And how does your life demonstrate and celebrate this reality?

Jesus, Son of God, let me be more appreciative of my family tree, and let me proudly proclaim myself as a child of God.

Live by the Spirit

> Live by the Spirit, I say, and do not gratify the desires of the flesh.
>
> (Galatians 5:16)

In this Scripture verse from Paul to the Galatians, Paul is offering particular guidelines on Christian living. He makes it very clear that one way to walk with Christ is to resist living by the desires of the flesh and having the "works of the flesh" dominate our lives. This does not mean that our body or our physical nature is bad. It simply means that our lives should be guided by the Spirit rather than by desires of the flesh. When our lives are ruled by the Spirit, we will experience such things as love, joy, peace, patience, kindness, generosity, faithfulness, gentleness, and self-control.

When my desires might separate me from you, O God, keep me on your path.

Positive Posting

> What is desirable in a person is loyalty,
>   and it is better to be poor than a liar.
>
> (Proverbs 19:22)

Using social networking sites and texting friends can be entertaining. However, it can provide a tempting opportunity to display false information. It is much easier to lie using a keyboard than to lie in person. Some lying may seem harmless: touching up a photo before posting it or saying you did something fun when you were really sitting at home. In fact, lying is never harmless and can even be dangerous. If we make accusations that may not be true, there can be dire consequences. Once a lie starts to travel electronically, we cannot stop its progress. Before texting or posting, let's be sure we are sharing something positive, communicating with truth, and acting with others' permission before we share something about them. We never know who will see what we write.

Lord, help me to always be mindful of the consequences of my behavior, both online and in person.

Don't Worry

> He said to his disciples, "Therefore I tell you,
> do not worry about your life, what you will eat,
> or about your body, what you will wear. For
> life is more than food, and the body more than
> clothing."
>
> (Luke 12:22–23)

Most of us have heard the song, "Don't Worry, Be Happy," which was released in 1988 and is still being recorded by various artists. As we listen or sing along, we may recall the Gospel message in this Scripture verse that is found in Luke. Jesus reminds us that worrying doesn't gain us anything. We should, instead, be more like birds or flowers, who don't worry about anything and yet are provided with all they need. Letting go and trusting in God can be difficult for us because we like to be in control. However, we must constantly remind ourselves that we are in God's hands. Doing our part, taking proper action, and preparing adequately are all important things that we must do, but ultimately we must learn to let go to God.

Help me, dear Lord, to let go of useless worry. Guide me to do what I can do, but then to trust in you.

Being a Blessing

> Do not repay evil for evil or abuse for abuse; but,
> on the contrary, repay with a blessing. It is for this
> you were called—that you might inherit a blessing.
>
> (1 Peter 3:9)

Repay evil with a blessing: really? Does this mean that when others treat us cruelly, or disrespectfully, we should pray for them and ask God to bless them? Yes! God calls us to be the better person. Being vengeful can lead to violence or abuse. The biblical advice to repay evil with a blessing may seem extraordinary to us. In fact, we know that many of Jesus' instructions seemed strange to his disciples, but they learned that actions and attitudes that often seem remarkable are indeed the path to God. As we practice the teaching to avoid repaying evil with evil, we too may learn how to stay on that path.

Help me to be like you, Jesus, especially when confronted with situations that might tempt me to react with violence.

Actions from Love

> Keep alert, stand firm in your faith, be courageous, be strong. Let all that you do be done in love.
>
> (1 Corinthians 16:13–14)

Being alert, standing firm in our faith, being courageous and strong is hard enough, but adding the instruction to do all that we do in love makes it even harder. But doing everything in love is a key component of our faith. We learn this through Scripture, at Mass, and in our families. Doing everything in love requires discipline and thought. Before taking action, it is helpful to ask: Why I am doing this? What is my real motivation? If the action is truly rooted in love and faith, we can be pretty sure that moving forward is a good idea. If other factors are influencing us, it is a good idea to revise our plan until Christian love is the motivator.

As I make decisions, Lord, I need your help so that all that I do is rooted in love.

Encouraging Faith

> Wife, for all you know, you might save your
> husband. Husband, for all you know, you might
> save your wife.
>
> (1 Corinthians 7:16)

If we replaced *wife* and *husband* with *girlfriend* and *boyfriend* in the above passage, we might also have wisdom for dating. Paul's instructions to the Corinthians concerned relationships among the early Christians. If we apply his advice to our modern lives, we can see how our lives might influence others, especially those closest to us, to be people of faith. Some of us may date people who are outside of our own faith tradition or people for whom faith is not an important part of life. We don't necessarily need to focus on getting the other person to believe as we do, but we should be able to freely talk about our own faith. Through our actions and through sharing our beliefs, we just may encourage someone to look more deeply at the role of faith in his or her own life.

Father of all, as I enter into relationships, let my faith be important enough to me to that I share it with others.

Faith and Confidence

"For how shall it be known that I have found favor in your sight, I and your people, unless you go with us?"

(Exodus 33:16)

Moses had a lot of doubt: doubt that he could speak, doubt that he could lead people, and doubt that people would listen to him. He called on God in times of doubt to gain strength and reassurance. Moses found out that he could rely on God and be very confident in his abilities because God would be with him. If we call on God and rely on him, we too can gain that confidence. We can develop a relationship with God that results in real faith and confidence. When filled with doubt, we can ask ourselves, Do I believe that God is pointing me in this direction? If he is, then he will certainly go with us.

God, my confidence, take away my doubt, and let me rely on you.

Wisdom or Money?

Happy are those who find wisdom,
   and those who get understanding,
for her income is better than silver,
   and her revenue better than gold.

(Proverbs 3:13–14)

If we pay attention to the media, we may hear the message that we should be working toward making money and storing up wealth. Magazines are filled with ads for expensive items, and TV shows and movies place popular products on the set and in the hands of the stars. Although there is nothing wrong with money or wealth, this proverb reminds us of the value of wisdom. Wisdom and understanding, we are told, are better than riches. Do you strive as much, if not more, for wisdom and understanding as you do to have the newest products? What objects do you place a high value on, and why?

God, source of all wisdom, help me to remember the things of real value.

School Attitude

> My brothers and sisters, whenever you face trials of any kind, consider it nothing but joy, because you know that the testing of your faith produces endurance.
>
> (James 1:2–3)

School can certainly feel like a trial. We might face being judged by our peers, and we face tests, athletic competitions, and time-consuming extracurricular activities. However, school also offers opportunities for joy. Instead of feeling judged by our peers, we can be joyful and stand up as good examples. As we approach tests and competitions, we can be joyful in the knowledge that each event helps us to learn and grow. We can face the demands of extracurricular activities with the joy of discovering passions that can help us to plot our future. As with many things in life, how we approach school determines if we'll be joyful. It is all in our attitude.

As I face the trials of school, I rely on you, Christ the teacher, to help me have a joyful attitude.

Overlook Faults

> Remember the commandments, and do not be
> angry with your neighbor; remember the covenant
> of the Most High, and overlook faults.
>
> (Sirach 28:7)

When someone does something that makes us angry, we usually do not think of God's promises first. We may even think about retaliation or revenge. The wise teacher and author of the book of Sirach gives us a difficult challenge when we're angry. When we are angered (and often also hurt), how can we overlook faults? How do we respond to anger in light of our faith? Scripture tells us that we do it by remembering God's promises. We may be more keenly aware of our anger and hurt than we are of our relationship with God, but that is part of the challenge we face as faith-filled people. The next time we are angry and tempted to get even, we can ask ourselves, What do I need to do to let go of this incident and move on with my faith journey?

Faithful and forgiving God, help me to overlook others' faults as you overlook mine.

Clear Mission

Then he said, "The God of our ancestors has chosen you to know his will, to see the Righteous One and to hear his own voice; for you will be his witness to all the world of what you have seen and heard."

(Acts of the Apostles 22:14–15)

This story of Paul's conversion is one we can turn to as an example of sticking to a commitment. Paul was given his sight back after being struck by a light from Heaven, then he was led to Damascus where he met a devout man who told him what his mission would be. Some people might have accepted healing and walked away, happy that they were over their illness or disease. Paul took his mission to heart and became one of the most important figures in the history of our faith. Our own call to serve may not be as clear as Paul's was, but we do know that whatever God calls us to do, we can accomplish, like Paul.

God, may my calling to serve you be clear, and may I follow through on it like Paul.

Ever Faithful God

> The steadfast love of the Lord never ceases,
>   his mercies never come to an end;
> they are new every morning;
>   great is your faithfulness.

(Lamentations 3:22–23)

A new start every morning with the love and mercy of God is a wonderful thing. We may have struggled throughout the day and faced all kinds of trouble and made mistakes, but we have a new day to look toward as we lay our head down on our pillow at night. If we have not been our best today, we can rely on the steadfast mercy of God, which is new every morning. If we need assurance of what faith can do for us, this part of Lamentations is a good reminder. No matter how bad our day, a reminder of God's faithfulness to us may be what we need to be faithful to God.

Merciful and ever loving Lord, as I face the trials of my life, I know you are here with me.

Words and Actions

"And I myself have seen and have testified that this is the Son of God."

(John 1:34)

Part of being a Christian is talking about Christ. John the Baptist, quoted above, gives his verbal testimony regarding Jesus. As followers of Christ, we can be like John the Baptist; we can tell others about Jesus and we can act like believers. For some of us, talking about our faith can be hard, so it might be good to come up with a few things to say about who we believe Jesus Christ to be. Equally, if not more important, we can show others what we believe by how we live. We can ask ourselves, What words and actions do I use to show and tell others about who Jesus is? When we can identify those words and actions easily, we will know we are testifying to Jesus Christ and his great love for us.

Christ, whom I follow, let me show and tell others of your greatness and love.

Forgiveness as Commanded

> Bear with one another and, if anyone has a
> complaint against another, forgive each other;
> just as the Lord has forgiven you, so you must also
> forgive.
>
> (Colossians 3:13)

"Bearing with one another" and "forgiving one another": those phrases give us a pretty good idea of what we are called to do as Christians. Most of us have experienced an action of another that has seemed unforgiveable. If a friend tells a secret we have shared in confidence or a family member has done something hurtful, we may feel we cannot possibly forgive. It can be helpful to ask ourselves: What if I had been the one who was hurtful? Wouldn't I want forgiveness? Whenever someone seeks our forgiveness and has the intention of not repeating the offense, it important to forgive them, just as God has forgiven us.

God, the great forgiver, help me to follow your example of forgiveness.

Supporting Others

Therefore we ought to support such people, so that we may become co-workers with the truth.

(3 John 1:8)

The "people" in this passage are those who traveled to spread the Gospel in the early days of the Church. Some of us may become involved in spreading the Good News as missionaries, possibly going to Africa to help those affected by war or to South America to teach in an underserved community. But even if we don't serve in this way, we all have the opportunity to help those who do. As we explore the issues of justice facing the world and our own community, we can seek out people who are serving others. When we find those people, we can support them. We might support their work materially through donations, food drives, or fund-raisers, or we might support their work through actions, such as organizing awareness events and letter-writing campaigns. We certainly can always help them through our prayers.

Christ, who inspires aid workers and volunteers of service, may I support the causes and people that support your mission.

Forgiveness Leading to Joy

> Be glad in the Lord and rejoice, O righteous,
>   and shout for joy, all you upright in heart.

> (Psalm 32:11)

We all sin and sometimes do things that separate us from God. But we are able to turn back to God to ask for forgiveness, to try to do better, and to learn from our sins. The psalmist David is joyful when he writes about those who have acknowledged their sin before God. He recognizes the beauty and peace that comes from forgiveness. God wants us to be happy and gives us an opportunity for happiness every day. Even if we choose to do something that separates us from our Creator, we can still be happy if we seek forgiveness. Are some areas in your life not joyful because you have separated yourself from God or others through your actions or thoughts? If we are honest in our answer, we can find the path to joyfulness.

God of love, may I continue to live in your joy.

Hope Lives On

> "If you love me, you will keep my commandments. And I will ask the Father, and he will give you another Advocate, to be with you forever."
>
> (John 14:15–16)

The followers of Jesus were able to spend time with him after the Resurrection, but he would eventually return to his Father. The night before he died, he told his disciples he would not be with them forever, but he also provided hope by promising the Holy Spirit (Advocate). He knew that his followers were going to need help and comfort when he was no longer physically with them. We also experience this hope in knowing that God is always with us, guiding and protecting us.

Holy Spirit, Hope and Advocate, I pray to you and ask that you cover me with comfort.

Love in Action

> Little children, let us love, not in word or speech,
> but in truth and action.
>
> (1 John 3:18)

It may be easier for us to say we love someone than to act like we do. We may say, "I love you" to a parent, but if we behave rudely toward them, or lie to them, we aren't loving them in truth and action. We may say we love our friends, but if we shun them at lunchtime or gossip about them, how can we say we love them? In order to love as Christians, we need to love in truth and action. We can ask ourselves: How do I show honor and respect to my parents? Do I accept my friends even if others shun them? Do I refrain from gossiping? Acting out of love means being kind and considerate—showing our love through the very way we live.

Loving God, your actions are evidence of your love for us. May we echo that love in our daily life.

Good People and Bad Things

> The Lord blessed the latter days of Job more than
> his beginning.
>
> (Job 42:12)

Sometimes we have to endure long periods of suffering. It could be that an entire semester of school is filled with trouble or that a certain year is rocky at home. Suffering can lead to a deeper appreciation of the good times. Job is a classic example of a man who suffered deeply through no fault of his own. We probably will not have to go through even a portion of what Job did, but we will nonetheless experience suffering. We may also see and hear of bad things happening to good people. Although we may not be able to understand these sufferings, we can remind ourselves of the end of Job's story. We can tell ourselves that we will be able to get through anything if we have faith and patience like Job.

Dear Lord, I will not try to figure out why bad things happen to good people. I will just pray through the suffering and look for the end of it in faith.

Popular Leaders

> Indeed from day to day people kept coming to
> David to help him, until there was a great army,
> like an army of God.
>
> (1 Chronicles 12:22)

David became a very popular leader. He achieved acclaim by doing things that his followers admired and by providing what they needed. He was charismatic and, most of all, he was faithful to God. He established a pattern of worship that was passed to many generations of believers. Jesus also used his popularity for good, healing the people and teaching them. If we become popular, we have the opportunity to use our popularity to bring people together or to divide them. As we have these opportunities, it's good to ask ourselves, In what ways can I use my popularity to be more like David and Jesus?

Dear God, help me to use my influence on others to be like our ancestors in faith and like your Son, Jesus, who used it for the good of all.

Accepting God's Challenge

> "So come, I will send you to Pharaoh to bring my
> people, the Israelites, out of Egypt." But Moses
> said to God, "Who am I that I should go to
> Pharaoh, and bring the Israelites out of Egypt?"
>
> (Exodus 3:10–11)

God challenges us at times to do things we do not think
we are capable or worthy of. We might think God
overestimates our abilities. But, as in Moses' case, God
knows exactly what we are able to do. God answered
Moses' question with, "I will be with you; and this shall be
the sign for you that it is I who sent you: when you have
brought the people out of Egypt, you shall worship God on
this mountain" (Exodus 3:12). Moses continued to accept
God's challenges. Although we might not be asked to do
things on the scale of Moses' achievements, God will most
certainly challenge us. When those challenges come, let's
make sure we're ready to answer, "Yes, Lord, here I am."

*Although I don't know what you may ask me to do, I
will always say, "Yes, Lord, here I am."*

Judith's Job

No one ever again spread terror among the Israelites during the lifetime of Judith, or for a long time after her death.

(Judith 16:25)

God calls people to serve in a variety of ways. As we read about Judith, we learn one story of how God might call people to greatness. This story of how Judith heard and answered God's call is a great one to turn to as we consider how to help our community. She responded to injustice in a courageous way and saved her people. Using her story as an example, we can look at our own communities and identify ways we can help. Judith spoke out and took action. For whom or what can you be a voice? How can you best serve your community as an answer to God's call?

God, who called Judith to greatness, call me and show me the ways I can help my community.

Maintain Justice

Thus says the Lord:
    Maintain justice, and do what is right,
for soon my salvation will come,
    and my deliverance be revealed.

(Isaiah 56:1)

Most of us like to understand what the standard is. In school we want to know how many points we need to get a good grade. In sports we want to know what skills we need to make the team. We want to know what our parents expect from us so we can be good family members. Scripture tells us what God expects: maintaining justice and doing what is right. We can work on meeting God's standards at any age. We can maintain justice at school by speaking out against a bully, or we can do what is right at home or with our friends. In all circumstances, we can learn to ask ourselves: Is this action helping to maintain justice? Is it right?

God, help me to maintain justice by doing what is right and setting an example for others.

Boundary-less Creation

And Ezra said: "You are the Lord, you alone; you have made heaven, the heaven of heavens, with all their host, the earth and all that is on it, the seas and all that is in them. To all of them you give life, and the host of heaven worships you."

(Nehemiah 9:6)

We may have boundaries around our homes, our cities, and our countries, but God's creation is over all. We can't draw a line and say that one group or one place is part of God's creation and another is not. The boundary of God's creation is endless, just like the boundary of God's love. As we make decisions about how we interact with creation, we need to ask ourselves: Will this action harm the air, the water, or the soil? Is there a consequence to this action for God's creation? If we are to honor God, who made the earth, we need to care for all of creation.

Lord, may I treat the earth and sea and sky with the care they deserve as part of your creation.

Symbols of Identity

> The Lord said to Moses: Speak to the Israelites,
> and tell them to make fringes on the corners of
> their garments throughout their generations and to
> put a blue cord on the fringe at each corner.
>
> (Numbers 15:37–38)

Some of us wear religious symbols, such as crosses or crucifixes. They identify us as Christians, and they also remind us how to act. The Old Testament Book of Numbers was written centuries before Christ was born, but this instruction to the Israelites is still followed by some Jewish people today. Men, and some women, wear these *tzitzits*, as they are called in Hebrew, on a particular garment. As they put the garment on, they pray a special blessing. We might do well to attach a special prayer to something we wear as a symbol and reminder of our Christian identity.

I wear outward symbols of my faith in you, O Lord: I pray that these symbols help me on the inside.

God's Love Reflected

How beautiful you are, my love,
  how very beautiful!

(Song of Solomon 4:1)

Being in love usually makes us feel good about ourselves. When someone likes us, we might stand a little taller and walk with a little more energy. We might write poetry expressing our happiness and high self-esteem. Likewise, when love is not returned, or when a relationship fails, we might keep our eyes on the ground and walk with slumped shoulders. Our poetry might be sad and full of lonely images. When we recognize God as one who loves us no matter what, and who will never break up with us, then we can always have the positive self-image that goes along with feelings of love. We don't need to wait for another person to tell us we're special, we just need to remember we are loved by God. When we remember this, we can stand tall. And when we do that, we are reflecting God's love to others.

God, who loves me no matter what, may I stand tall with that love.

Acceptable Hearts

> But the Lord said to Samuel, "Do not look on
> his appearance or on the height of his stature,
> because I have rejected him; for the Lord does
> not see as mortals see; they look on the outward
> appearance, but the Lord looks on the heart."
>
> (1 Samuel 16:7)

We may think we need to look a certain way to fit in
with our peers. We may try to look like those who are
popular as a way to gain acceptance. Trying to look like
someone else may lead others to accept us at first, but the
most important acceptance is acceptance of who we truly
are—the kind of acceptance that comes from God. God
doesn't accept us for how we look but for what is in our
heart. Are you working too hard on achieving a certain
look just to fit in? Are you working enough on what is
important to God—what is in your heart?

*Lord, who loves me no matter what, I pray that my
heart is acceptable to you.*

Two by Two

> After this the Lord appointed seventy others and sent them on ahead of him in pairs to every town and place where he himself intended to go.
>
> (Luke 10:1)

When we have a hard job to do or a big project to complete, we can often make the work easier by recruiting a partner. When we have friends who partner with us for success, we learn about give and take. When our friends are in need of help, we are there to support them. And if we are the one who needs help, our friends are there for us. When Jesus sent his disciples out, he knew the power of partnering. As we choose friends, we might ask ourselves: Will this person put as much into the friendship as he or she receives from it? If I need help in school or at home, is this friend the type who will help me? Will this person support my faith?

I ask that you breathe love and partnership into my friendships, Holy Spirit.

What's My Motivation?

> Am I now seeking human approval, or God's
> approval? Or am I trying to please people? If
> I were still pleasing people, I would not be a
> servant of Christ.

> (Galatians 1:10)

We might feel like Paul sometimes as we try to figure out our motives. We might think we're doing something with good intentions, but then we may question whether we are just trying to please people. We may feel confused as we try to decide the answers to questions like these: Am I doing this because it will look good to others? Does this action truly reflect what I believe is best? What is motivating me to do this? As we take our relationship with Christ more seriously and begin to act on it, we may find that others question our behavior. However, if our intention is to be a servant of Christ, the approval of others will not be our primary concern.

Christ, I seek to be your servant. Let me be sincere in my words and actions.

Listen to Your Father

> Listen, children, to a father's instruction,
>   and be attentive, that you may gain insight;
> for I give you good precepts:
>   do not forsake my teaching.
>
> (Proverbs 4:1–2)

Most of us have had a parent say to us, "Listen to me!" and then tell us something that we think is unimportant. But when we really listen to our parents' instructions, we just might gain an insight we would have otherwise missed. Our parents have had experiences we can learn from. If we listen carefully to what they are trying to teach us, we can often find a deeper meaning. As we get instructions from our parents, we can remind ourselves to listen and learn. Instead of tuning them out, we can do as this proverb suggests: be attentive and gain insight.

Your instructions are opportunities for me to learn, O God. Help me to remember that about my parents as they give me instructions and offer their insights.

Self-Control

> Do not follow your base desires, but restrain your appetites.
>
> (Sirach 18:30)

It is easy to give in to temptation. Every day, we face decisions that can help or hurt or relationship with God. Ben Sira soundly advised us not to give in to our base desires. These are attitudes and practices that include laziness, drunkenness, and lust, which might bring some immediate pleasure but also lead to long-term problems. Self-control is the strength to resist the lusts that lead to lifelong problems. What base desires tempt you the most? What do you need to do to strengthen your self-control and avoid having base desires and appetites rule your life?

God of love, I may be tempted, but help me to have self-control and to keep myself focused on the long-term goal of leading a healthy and happy life.

Build Instead of Bully

> Therefore encourage one another and build up
> each other, as indeed you are doing.
>
> (1 Thessalonians 5:11)

The instructions Paul gives the Thessalonians were pertinent to their times and are still meaningful for us today. However, Paul might add to these instructions, reminding us that they apply to our use of technology as well. He would likely remind us not to participate in cyberbullying and instead to use technology to offer one another support. So although the time may be different, the point is the same. We are called to encourage and affirm one another, and most of us, like the Thessalonians, are doing just that. It can still be helpful, before hitting "send" or "enter" on our keypad, to ask ourselves: Does this text or e-mail build someone up or tear someone down? If others see this text or e-mail, might I regret what I send or say?

If I could text you, God, I'd praise your name and tell you how I'm building others up.

Safety and Security

> Although you have not seen him, you love him;
> and even though you do not see him now, you
> believe in him and rejoice with an indescribable
> and glorious joy, for you are receiving the
> outcome of your faith, the salvation of your souls.
>
> (1 Peter 1:8–9)

For most of us, we rely on a certain level of safety and security, knowing our friends and parents are there to help us, guide us, and provide support for us. We might even say we have faith in our loved ones: we trust them and feel certain of their love and care for us. These people, whom we see, can give us a sense of the security and safety that can be found in God, whom we do not see. When we need to feel safe, we only need to rely on our faith. As we learn to trust more deeply in God's love, we will feel incredible joy and ultimately receive the outcome of our faith, the salvation of our soul.

I don't see you, God, but I have faith in you, my courage and my salvation.

Don't Be Silent

> And have mercy on some who are wavering; save others by snatching them out of the fire; and have mercy on still others with fear.
>
> (Jude 1:22–23)

When our peers go off in a wrong direction, we can talk with them or find a responsible, caring adult to help. The writer of the letter to Jude advised the Christian community about people who might take them off the path of faithfulness: those who doubt their faith, those who reject godly ways, and those who are so afraid of sin that they live in fear. Today we know people just like them. We can help those who doubt or those who are fearful by listening and sharing our own beliefs. When we see our peers doing something wrong, we can help them without judging. If their behavior is harmful or illegal, we need to find an adult who can help. Instead of condemning those who reject God's ways, we can pray for them.

Holy Spirit, I ask for the courage to help or get help for others without condemning them.

Doers of the Word

> But be doers of the word, and not merely hearers
> who deceive themselves.
>
> (James 1:22)

We hear the Word of God at Mass every Sunday, in our religion classes, at Confirmation preparation sessions, or in our youth groups, but do we always respond with our actions? Sometimes we hear the words, but perhaps we're thinking of what we're going to do when we get home or we're whispering to our friends or texting. Although the Word of God may seem boring to us, it is important that we figure out what it is calling us to do. We have to reach beyond just hearing the words to becoming "doers of the word." As we truly listen to the Word of God, it can be helpful to ask ourselves: What is the Word of God calling me to today? How do the words I am hearing today help me to know what to do tomorrow?

Open my ears, Lord, so that I may hear, and open my mind so that I may know what to do to follow in your footsteps.

Patient and Gentle Relationships

> I . . . beg you to lead a life worthy of the calling
> to which you have been called, with all humility
> and gentleness, with patience, bearing with one
> another in love. . . .
>
> (Ephesians 4:1–2)

As Christians we are called to demonstrate all of the characteristics we read about in the above verse from the Letter to the Ephesians. And if we are living the life to which we have been called, these characteristics will be shown in all areas of our life. As we begin developing new relationships with others, these should be some of the key qualities that are present. It can be helpful to reflect on how humility, gentleness, patience, and love are shown in the variety of relationships we have. It can also be helpful to ask ourselves how we are actively working to ensure the presence of these qualities.

God whose love is perfect in all things, I know I am not perfect in all my relationships, but in your love I know I can be all that you call me to be.

No Shrinking Back

> But we are not among those who shrink back and
> so are lost, but among those who have faith and
> so are saved.
>
> (Hebrews 10:39)

If we doubt, we shrink back and feel lost. We lose
courage and find it hard to draw on our faith. But faith
can give us courage. We can rest in the knowledge that
our faith saves us and gives us the strength we need to
respond to God's call in our lives. As we find ourselves
shrinking back because we are not confident in our faith,
we can recall the words of the Letter to the Hebrews and
remind ourselves that our faith will lead us forward. Like
the Hebrews, we are called to be strong and not to shrink
back in fear.

*Help me, Jesus Christ, my strength and courage, to
overcome my doubts and fears.*

Anxiety over Money

> Wakefulness over wealth wastes away one's flesh,
> and anxiety about it drives away sleep.
>
> (Sirach 31:1)

Some of us become obsessed about making money or having a lot of things. Although we need money, it is important that we avoid becoming overly concerned with it. If we continue reading the Wisdom of Sirach, we learn more about the right attitude toward riches. Money is necessary, but it can be a deterrent to more Godly pursuits and a stumbling block on our path of faithfulness. It can even lead to our ruin. As we begin to decide how to use our birthday or holiday gifts of money or the money we earn, we are advised to not let anxiety consume us. As we become more in control of our own money and wealth, we can ask, Am I paying more attention to money and wealth than to my relationships and experiences?

God of all riches, keep my mind focused on the things and people that are important.

Grace and Self-Discipline

> For this reason I remind you to rekindle the gift of God that is within you through the laying on of my hands: for God did not give us a spirit of cowardice, but rather a spirit of power and of love and of self-discipline.

> (2 Timothy 1:6–7)

One reason some of us stress out about school is that we do not have a plan or do not stick to a study schedule. When we start off a school year or a new semester, we might be disciplined and determined, but within a few weeks we might get bogged down or lose discipline. In order to maintain a schedule, we really need to have a spirit of self-discipline. Two Sacraments we have likely celebrated—Baptism and Confirmation—involve the laying on of hands. Through the laying on of hands, the Holy Spirit is poured out to be our helper and guide, and we are given various Gifts of the Holy Spirit that strengthen us for our lives of faith. Let us use these gifts to strengthen our spirit of power, love, and self-discipline.

Help me to remember your grace, God of discipline and of power and of love.

Hatred into Love

Hatred stirs up strife, but love covers all offenses.

(Proverbs 10:12)

We may get angry at someone if they've hurt us or harmed someone we love. Anger is an acceptable emotion, but when we're very angry it is a good idea to have a trusted adult to turn to. If anger turns to hatred, we may face consequences we aren't ready to handle. If we are angry, it can be particularly helpful to talk to someone who is not involved in the situation to help us work through our anger. If anger starts to become hatred, we need to ask ourselves: Why am I so angry? What can I do to find the love in this situation? Can I talk to someone who would be objective and can help me turn the hatred into love?

God of love, help me to know the signs of anger and hatred and to get the help I need when I am experiencing these feelings.

Why Keep Commitments?

"For whoever does the will of my Father in heaven is my brother and sister and mother."

(Matthew 12:50)

Making and keeping commitments is an important part of life and provides opportunities for us to grow. Keeping a commitment to a parent might result in more freedom because we have proven ourselves to be trustworthy. Keeping a commitment to school or to a teacher might improve our grades. Keeping a commitment to ourselves, such as the commitment to practice something more, helps us to become better at the skill or activity in which we are participating. Keeping a commitment to Jesus and to following God's will helps us to grow as part of the family of God. If we are having trouble keeping commitments, we can ask ourselves: How will others benefit if I keep my commitments? How does keeping commitments benefit my own growth? If we can recognize the benefits, we may grow in our ability to keep our commitments.

Jesus, my brother, may I learn to keep all my commitments, especially the ones I make to you.

Daniel's Courage and Faithfulness

> Then the king gave the command, and Daniel
> was brought and thrown into the den of lions. The
> king said to Daniel, "May your God, whom you
> faithfully serve, deliver you!"
>
> (Daniel 6:16)

We will hopefully never have to face a den of lions, but we will all experience times when we need to have courage. We may have to face a bully, an angry peer, or some other uncomfortable situation. In these moments we know we can call on God. Daniel's story highlights the theme of God's care and protection for his faithful. Daniel called on God with absolute trust, and the king released him the next day. If we are faced with a situation that frightens us, we can call on God for strength as we remember the story of Daniel in the lion's den.

Lord, I pray to have Daniel's courage and wisdom.

Walk in Love

> And this is love, that we walk according to his commandments; this is the commandment just as you have heard it from the beginning—you must walk in it.
>
> (2 John 1:6)

The idea of walking in love may sound romantic to us. We don't know what it sounded like to the early Christians, but we do know it had to be explained to them. The explanation works for us too: love is not solely about romance, but about walking according to God's commandments. As we know, the Ten Commandments are very specific about the way we are to live and add up to a way of life that we can sum up in one word: *love*. In almost any situation, we can benefit from asking ourselves, How can I walk according to the Ten Commandments and truly love?

I want to walk in your love, Creator God. Help me to know and to walk this path.

Sin and Forgiveness

And forgive us our sins, for we ourselves forgive everyone indebted to us.

(Luke 11:4)

We are human, and humans make mistakes and sin. Some mistakes are more like accidents and some are the result of bad decisions. There is a difference between a mistake and a sin, however, and we usually can tell the difference. When we make mistakes, we need to apologize and do what we can to correct the mistake. But when we deliberately choose to do something we know is morally wrong, that is a sin. When we sin, we still need to apologize and deal with the consequences of our actions, but we also need to ask for God's forgiveness. With the help of the Holy Spirit, we can learn from our sins and find the strength to avoid repeating them.

Help me, forgiving God, to make the right choices and to seek reconciliation when I fail to do so.

Jesus and Service

"Today this scripture has been fulfilled in your hearing."

(Luke 4:21)

Jesus spoke these words after he read words from Isaiah about bringing good news to the poor and letting the oppressed go free. We know that doing good deeds and striving for justice is the right thing to do. Not only does it feel good to help someone else, but we know that service is part of how a community functions. What is important to remember is that service is a key part of our Christian mission. Scripture helps us to understand how Jesus' mission was directly connected to the service to others. As we reflect on the ways that Jesus served others and brought good news to the poor, we can be inspired to have the same focus on service in our own lives.

Lord, I am called to participate in and continue your mission. May your example remind me of my own call to serve others.

Rejoice in the Lord

Finally, my brothers and sisters, rejoice in the Lord.

(Philippians 3:1)

When we rejoice, we express our happiness. But sometimes it seems as if happiness came easier when we were younger. Sometimes as we get older, we find it harder to be happy. We feel more pressures, we encounter negative experiences, and it seems as if we don't have as much time to enjoy simple things. When we find it hard to discover happiness, we might want to turn to the Lord. No matter what is going on in our lives, God is there. The Holy Spirit surrounds us and Christ our brother is by our side. If we can't find anything to rejoice in, we can ask ourselves, How can I stop for a few minutes and just be with God? Then we need to do whatever it takes to find those moments of quiet. When we do, we can rejoice in the Lord.

Father, Son, and Holy Spirit, be with me and let me feel the happiness I seek.

A Time for Everything

> For everything there is a season, and a time for
> every matter under heaven.
>
> (Ecclesiastes 3:1)

We know that we all experience both good times and
bad times. We also know that sometimes we want to be
around people, while other times we want to be alone.
At other times, we may feel happy and joyful or we may
feel distressed or sad. There does seem to be a "season"
for everything. When we are sad or feeling hopeless, it is
reassuring to know that there will be a time when we will
again be happy. If we are mourning the death of a loved
one or going through a difficult time right now, perhaps
we can find some comfort in this part of Ecclesiastes. It is
a helpful passage that can bring us hope.

*Help me, Lord, to resist running away from my
feelings. If I am feeling sad or distressed, help me
to know that happiness and peace will eventually be
mine.*

Steadfast Love

> O give thanks to the Lord, for he is good,
>   for his steadfast love endures forever.
>
>   (Psalm 136:1)

Sometimes we experience days when we feel as if no one loves us. Maybe we've had a day when our parents were angry with us, our teachers would not listen to us, our friends were all busy, and even the dog didn't seem interested in hanging out! It can help to know that even on our very worst days, God loves us. God loves us, as the psalmist says, forever. So the next time we're having "one of those days," we can remind ourselves of the answer to the question, "Doesn't anyone love me?" The answer is: Yes, God does, and his steadfast love endures forever.

Thank you, God, for your steadfast love. Help me to remember it, even on the worst days.

You Are Blessed in Suffering

Now who will harm you if you are eager to do what is good? But even if you do suffer for doing what is right, you are blessed.

(1 Peter 3:13–14)

We who are eager to do good might sometimes get called names. Although name-calling does not harm us physically, it still hurts. Losing people we thought were friends when we try to do good is especially hard. The author of this New Testament letter knew that the early Christians faced that type of verbal harm; some even faced physical harm. He encourages them, and us, to continue doing what is good. He reminds us that we are blessed when we suffer taunts or are shunned for what is right.

Christ Jesus, who suffered both physical and verbal harm, help me continue to follow your way, even when others try to make me feel bad for doing good.

Good Advice?

> Let those who are friendly with you be many, but
> let your advisers be one in a thousand.

> (Sirach 6:6)

We may have a lot of friends both in person and online. When we have many people around us, we must know which ones to turn to for advice. Some people who give us advice may be doing it not for us but for themselves; they may advise us to do something so they look better or may even tell us to do something that makes us look bad. Before we turn to someone for advice, we might want to ask ourselves: What actions does this person take that I admire? Does this person have the experience and wisdom to advise me? Will she or he have my best interest in mind?

As my friend, Christ Jesus, you know what is best. I pray that the Holy Spirit will inspire my advisers. And may all advice given to me be that which comes from God.

Our Father

> "Pray then in this way: Our Father in heaven,
> hallowed be your name."
>
> (Matthew 6:9)

Many of us think of God as Father. Jesus invites us to use that term as he did because he wants others to know of the relationship he had with God and to share in it. If we haven't had a good relationship with our own fathers, we might not understand Jesus' use of this word. Praying to God as Father can reinforce the positive image of fathers some of us have and can provide a better image of fathers for others. The next time we pray the Lord's Prayer, we can focus on the words *Our Father* and know that God is a good and faithful Father for all of us.

Our Father, I pray to you with the words Jesus invited us to use. Help me to know the loving care you have for me.

Jonah's Call

> Now the word of the Lord came to Jonah son
> of Amittai, saying, "Go at once to Nineveh,
> that great city, and cry out against it: for their
> wickedness has come up before me." But Jonah
> set out to flee to Tarshish from the presence of the
> Lord.
>
> (Jonah 1:1–3)

We've all had the experience of ignoring a parent, a teacher, or a coach who was calling our name. Maybe we know our mother was going to tell us to do a chore, the teacher was going to ask a question we weren't prepared to answer, or the coach wanted us to use a skill we hadn't mastered. Usually we end up with some sort of consequence for our choice of ignoring them: extra chores, extra homework, or extra laps. Jonah is like that too; he heard God's messenger and did not do what he was told. Jonah suffered the consequence of his actions and didn't like what happened to him. But he learned his lesson and followed God's Word the next time God called. We can learn from his mistakes.

God who calls me, let me hear your voice and do your will.

Working toward Peace

> He shall judge between the nations,
>   and shall arbitrate for many peoples;
> they shall beat their swords into plowshares,
>   and their spears into pruning hooks;
> nation shall not lift up sword against nation,
>   neither shall they learn war anymore.
>
> (Isaiah 2:4)

As we see reports about war in the news, we learn that peace sometimes comes when there are arbitrators. Arbitrators work to find a solution that is most just. Sometimes an objective person can design a solution to meet the needs of both sides. What can you do to mediate peace among your friends? How can you support peace efforts for our world through your everyday actions? When we work for peace, we participate in God's will for the world.

O Perfect Peace, great arbitrator, make me a part of the work of creating a peace-filled earth.

Time for Fallow Ground

> For six years you shall sow your land and gather in its yield; but on the seventh year you shall let it rest and lie fallow.
>
> (Exodus 23:10–11)

We know that the earth has limited resources. Farmers understand the need for crop rotation and for allowing their fields to rest before replanting. This gives the ground a chance to regain its ability to provide nutrients to the plants. In ancient times, God's Law instructed the people of God to let the ground lay fallow. Future generations benefited from this practice. Many individuals and organizations today work to conserve nature and protect our water, air, and earth. As we reflect on God's concern that we care for the earth, we can ask ourselves, What can I do to help preserve the natural world for future generations?

God, help me to protect the earth so it will benefit future generations.

Who Knows Me?

> [The Lord] formed me in the womb to be his
>   servant,
> to bring Jacob back to him,
>   and that Israel might be gathered to him,
> for I am honored in the sight of the Lord,
>   and my God has become my strength.
>
> (Isaiah 49:5)

It is a common experience to wonder about our identity:
our place in our family, how we fit in at school, or what
gifts we have to offer to the world. We also may find that
we frequently wonder about who we are supposed to be
in the world and what we're supposed to do. God knows
our identity completely. As we hear in Isaiah, God forms
us to be his servant. If we remember that the starting point
of our identity is to be God's servant, we can use that
knowledge to help us answer further questions about who
we are and what we are meant to do.

*God, you formed me and you know me; help me to
know myself.*

Chosen Ones

> As God's chosen ones, holy and beloved, clothe
> yourselves with compassion, kindness, humility,
> meekness, and patience.
>
> (Colossians 3:12)

It can be difficult to fully understand that we are chosen
and loved by God. Because we are chosen by God,
we are called to act with compassion, kindness,
humility, meekness, and patience. By developing these
characteristics in ourselves, we honor who we are as
God's chosen ones. It's helpful then, when in times of
doubt about our self-worth, to remember these words from
the Letter to the Colossians and to hold ourselves at the
same level of esteem God does. Do you really believe
God holds you in high esteem? How do your actions
reveal to others your holiness and that you are loved by
God? How might your acts of compassion and kindness
help someone else experience her or his own worth?

*God, help me to remember that I am loved and that
I can help others know their worth by treating them
with compassion and kindness.*

Standing Firm

> "This Jesus is 'the stone that was rejected by you, the builders, it has become the cornerstone.'"
>
> (Acts of the Apostles 4:11)

At times we may feel rejected by those closest to us. Sometimes our families don't accept us when we are trying to discover who we are. Sometimes we feel rejected by our friends, especially if they are going in a direction we don't want to take. It doesn't feel good to be rejected, but we can find comfort in knowing that Jesus was rejected too. Jesus didn't veer from his mission even amid the rejection. He stood firm in his identity as God's beloved Son. As we reflect on how Jesus withstood rejection, we can ask ourselves if we can stand firm in the knowledge that even when we feel rejected we are following in Jesus' footsteps.

Jesus, some of those near you rejected you. May I draw on your strength when I am feeling rejected.

Thankful for Friends

> I have indeed received much joy and encouragement from your love, because the hearts of the saints have been refreshed through you, my brother.

> (Philemon 1:7)

Good friends help us to be more joyful. If someone does the opposite of this by filling us with anxiety or sadness, it could be that he or she needs help, or it could be that we need to reevaluate our friendship. As we think of our friends and reflect on Paul's words to Philemon, we can help evaluate our friendships by seeing if we can put our friend's name in place of "my brother." If we can place our friend's name in the above Scripture and the statement is true, we know we have found a friend who will be a positive influence in our life.

Thank you, generous God, for those friends who bring joy to my life and help me to share in your Good News.

Wary of Advice

> All counselors praise the counsel they give,
>   but some give counsel in their own interest.
> Be wary of a counselor,
>   and learn first what is his interest,
>   for he will take thought for himself.
>
> (Sirach 37:7–9)

"Come on. I did it and it was ok!" "If I were you, I'd do this." "I told someone else to do it this way, and he loved my advice." When you hear statements like these, you may have met a "counselor" who praises his own advice. Wisdom teaches us to be careful when someone gives us advice. Some advice givers want to justify their own behavior by convincing us to go along. Others may feel self-important when they make decisions for everyone around them. Those of our peers who give good advice do it out of an interest for our well-being rather than their own.

As I learn to listen to others' advice, may I know the intention of the advice giver and be grateful for those friends who help me to follow you, my God and guide.

Listen and Accept

> Hear, my child, your father's instruction,
>   and do not reject your mother's teaching;
> for they are a fair garland for your head,
>   and pendants for your neck.
>
> (Proverbs 1:8–9)

We don't always want to hear our father's advice or always think our mother has something to teach us. Sometimes we might even be tempted to just do the opposite of what they say, and we may not listen as closely as we could. As parents give us instruction and teaching, we are well advised by the writer of the Proverbs to "hear" and "not reject" them. This doesn't necessarily mean we will always agree with what they are saying. It does mean, however, that we won't immediately dismiss what they are saying due to a lack of respect. It is important to really listen to our parents, knowing that their advice often contains "jewels" of wisdom that are meant to help us.

God, whom I honor as Father, let me honor my earthly parents by listening to them and accepting their wisdom.

Clear Instructions

> Put to death, therefore, whatever in you is earthly: fornication, impurity, passion, evil desire, and greed (which is idolatry).
>
> (Colossians 3:5)

It is quite helpful to have clear and easy-to-understand guidelines. Such instructions might come to us from a parent, a teacher, a coach, or from Scripture or the Church's Tradition. The instructions given to the Colossians regarding sexual activity in today's Scripture verse couldn't be easier to understand. Paul makes it very clear that sexual impurity is not part of the plan as we follow Christ. We don't have to take a lot of time or energy to figure out Paul's instruction in this passage. His forthrightness allows us to easily discern what we should do to keep ourselves holy and pure.

Thank you, God, for the gift of your Word that lets us know so clearly what and who we are called to be.

Tame the Tongue and the Text

> But no one can tame the tongue—a restless evil,
> full of deadly poison. With it we bless the Lord
> and Father, and with it we curse those who are
> made in the likeness of God.

> (James 3:8–9)

Most of us have used words at one point or another that we'd like to take back. Unfortunately, once we say something out loud, we put it out for all to hear. Likewise, when we write something and text it, or post it to a Web page, we put it out in the world. If this writer were sending his epistle today, he might replace the word *tongue* with *keyboard*. Christ's early followers apparently had just as much trouble with words as we do. Learning to think before we speak or write is a difficult task, but if we can just remember to ask ourselves if the words we are speaking or writing are meant to uplift or tear down, we may save ourselves regret.

Lord, whom I long to praise, let only words that please you come from my lips and fingertips.

The Lord as Guard

> But the Lord is faithful; he will strengthen you and guard you from the evil one.
>
> (2 Thessalonians 3:3)

If we ask ourselves where we see "the evil one" in our lives, what would be our answer? All of us sin, and most of us face a particular temptation that we know goes against God's desire for us. These things may be hard to stay away from or stop doing. But God keeps us safe from these evils if we call out and ask for help. Sometimes that help might come in the form of another person, like a caring adult who can assist us in getting the help we need or a friend who sets a good example. The help might also come in the form of positive activities that can take the place of the sinful ones in our lives. These are some of the ways God keeps us safe.

God, my shelter, help me to find safety from the evil one in my life.

Deliver Me

Deliver me, O Lord, from evildoers;
    protect me from those who are violent,
who plan evil things in their minds
    and stir up wars continually.

(Psalm 140:1–2)

Sometimes other students at school are trying to stir things up. They might intentionally cause conflict by gossiping about others or try to start a fight or encourage violence. It's good to be alert to what might be brewing, and to let caring, responsible adults know if we hear something suspicious. If we overhear a harmful plan of violence or bullying, or even hear a rumor about one, we need to ask ourselves questions like, these: What would happen if this is true? Can I prevent harm by letting someone in authority know about this?

As I become aware of plans that sound harmful, may you, God my confidant, protect me and help me know when to notify someone in authority.

Live in the Spirit

> If we live by the Spirit, let us also be guided by
> the Spirit. Let us not become conceited, competing
> against one another, envying one another.
>
> (Galatians 5:25–26)

If someone were to ask some of your classmates or family members if your actions demonstrate that you live by the Spirit and are guided by the Spirit, what do you think they would say? Would they say you live by faith? Faith helps us to think highly of others instead of regarding ourselves as superior; it encourages us to help others achieve success instead of striving to outdo them; it enables us to admire others instead of feeling jealous. Living by faith lets us know how to live our values, and gives us a benchmark to check ourselves against. If we allow the Spirit to guide us, we can be assured of living by Christ's designs.

Holy Spirit, guide me so that my actions may truly reflect the faith and values I want to live by.

God as Matchmaker?

> "Ask, and it will be given you; search, and you will find; knock, and the door will be opened for you."
>
> (Matthew 7:7)

We might want a boyfriend or a girlfriend so badly that we do silly things to attract one. But perhaps we should take this prayer to God. What if we asked God to help us find the right person when we are fully prepared to begin dating? By keeping God in the process of finding a special person, we may be more likely to remember that it is important to surround ourselves by people who support us, who want the best for us, and who encourage us in our faith. When we ask God for help in anything, he will respond. But we must have open eyes and open hearts to receive his response, whatever that may be.

God, I trust that you are with me in all of my decisions and actions. Help me to surround myself by people who support, encourage, and like me for who I am.

Is It Possible?

> Jesus answered them, "Truly I tell you, if you have faith and do not doubt . . . even if you say to this mountain, 'Be lifted up and thrown into the sea,' it will be done. Whatever you ask for in prayer with faith, you will receive."
>
> (Matthew 21:21–22)

If we tell a mountain to throw itself in the sea, do we really think it will happen? If we ask God to help us, do we really think God will follow through? Is there any difference between the two requests? In God's sight there is not. We are the ones who start to doubt and question whether we have enough faith. As soon as we start doubting, we become unable to do the great things God allows us to do with faith. Although we won't want to throw a mountain into the sea, there will be things we want to do. Keeping our faith strong helps us to do those things that seem impossible; with God they are possible.

May I erase all doubt in you, Lord God, so that I may accomplish great things through faith.

A Love of Money

> Keep your lives free from the love of money, and
> be content with what you have.
>
> (Hebrews 13:5)

We are reliant on money. Without it we cannot provide for our basic needs of shelter, food, and clothing. Without money, higher education may be out of reach. Money is also the root of many conflicts, problems, and worries. Are you letting your love of money overrule your love of others? Is anxiety over money causing you to lose sight of what is most important to you? Do you try to have more and more, rather than allowing what you have to be enough? We will all do well to listen to the advice we find in the Letter to the Hebrews.

Christ Jesus, you were born a poor child and were never trapped by a desire for material things. Help me to be more like you, free from an unhealthy love of money.

Stress Free?

> So do not worry about tomorrow, for tomorrow
> will bring worries of its own. Today's trouble is
> enough for today.
>
> (Matthew 6:34)

Jesus obviously didn't live in the twentieth century. How can we not be anxious in these busy times? Nonetheless, Jesus tells us not to worry. Jesus does not ask us not to think about tomorrow, but rather not to be anxious about it. It's easy to get so stressed out over a big test that we start getting stressed about everything else. Here is wisdom: pay attention to one day at a time. Prepare for the test but don't stress. Stay focused, and pray for strength, wisdom, and peace.

Gentle God, it's easy to become obsessed with the details of my life. Help me to keep them in focus and always to turn to you for guidance and strength.

Slow to Anger

> Whoever is slow to anger has great understanding,
> but one who has a hasty temper exalts folly.
>
> (Proverbs 14:29)

Many of us get angry quickly and without thinking. Sometimes we scheme as a way to get back at someone who has hurt us. Acting quickly and out of anger is rarely wise: we may hurt others, and we give others a reason to dislike us. We can stop and think when we are angry, and ask ourselves: Why am I so angry? What can I do in a Christian, holy way that can help to address this anger I'm feeling? If we pause, instead of acting quickly without thinking, we buffer the haste that may lead to behavior we know is foolish.

Lord, help me to slow down and think before acting, especially when I'm angry. Help me to be a person of great understanding and patience, slow to anger.

Faithful and Sincere Commitments

"Now therefore revere the Lord, and serve him in sincerity and in faithfulness."

(Joshua 24:14)

When others give us instructions, we have two options. One option is to do what they say while we grumble and only do the minimal requirements. The other option is to follow the instructions carefully while we try to do our best. When we make a commitment, whether to a class, a parent, a boss, or anyone in authority, we promise to follow through in a spirit of sincerity and faithfulness. Before making commitments, we can ask ourselves questions like these: Do I have the time to commit to this project, job, or schedule? Will I regret taking on this responsibility?

God of all faithfulness, whose commitments are most sincere, help me to be sincere and faithful as I make commitments.

Cast Anxiety on God

Cast all your anxiety on him, because he cares for
you.

(1 Peter 5:7)

When we are worried or anxious, we might hold our
breath, waiting to see what will happen. Knowing that
someone cares for us can allow us to exhale. It has a
calming effect on our anxiety and helps to spread the
anxiety thinner while creating a sense of peace. We can
find out who best to surround ourselves with when we
are anxious by asking ourselves, Who are those people
who care for me and who I can talk to about the things
that worry me? Knowing who those people are is a great
help. Knowing that God cares for us is an even greater
help. It is like having a friend that is always available to
us. This ability to cast our anxiety on God can lead to a
deep peace and a lessening of anxiety.

*I know you are here, God, and I place this anxiety at
your feet. Guide me to peace, and let me feel your
loving care.*

Remembrance of Christ

> Then he took a loaf of bread, and when he had
> given thanks, he broke it and gave it to them,
> saying, "This is my body which is given for you.
> Do this in remembrance of me."
>
> (Luke 22:19)

To celebrate the Eucharist is to commit ourselves to a way of life based on the life, Passion, death, and Resurrection of Jesus. Over and over again, we commit ourselves to dying to self and living for others, to putting to death our old ways of sin and living a life of holiness, to embracing the cross so that we might be raised to new life in Christ. Each week, we strive to live more like Christ. The command, "Do this in remembrance of me," is one of the most important instructions Jesus gave. The next time we're at Mass and hear the priest say these words in the Liturgy of the Eucharist, we can reflect on how important it is for us to remember Jesus in this way and to live more fully as Christians.

*Christ, our sacrifice, help me to know the importance
of the Eucharist in my life.*

Return and Ask

> Take words with you
>   and return to the Lord;
> say to him,
>   "Take away all guilt:
> accept that which is good,
>   and we will offer
>   the fruit of our lips."
>
> (Hosea 14:2)

When we are sorry for hurting a friend, we go back to that person and use words that reflect our desire for forgiveness. So it is with our relationship with God, according to the Prophet Hosea. When we have strayed, it is important to "return" to him and "take words" with us that express our desire for forgiveness. Repentance requires true sorrow and our asking God to change our heart. It leads to an active response to make amends with God and with the Church. Such repentance is called reconciliation, and Catholics celebrate it in the Sacrament of Penance and Reconciliation. When was the last time you experienced God's love and mercy in the Sacrament of Penance and Reconciliation? Even if it has been awhile, God and the Church are always there waiting with open arms.

Forgiving God, help me to acknowledge those times I have sinned, and help me to return to you, using my words to seek forgiveness.

Love the Stranger

> For the Lord . . . executes justice for the orphan
> and the widow, and . . . loves the strangers,
> providing them food and clothing. You shall also
> love the stranger, for you were strangers in the
> land of Egypt.
>
> (Deuteronomy 10:17–19)

When we take part in a food drive or other service project
to help people who are very much like ourselves, the help
we give seems natural. We can imagine ourselves in their
situation. When we help someone who is a "stranger,"
different from us because of culture, ethnicity, or religion,
we are reminded that we have been strangers at times as
well. We realize that although others may seem different
from us, we share the same basic needs. When we ask
ourselves, How should I treat those who are strangers? the
answer is clear: We need to love them and be of service
to them.

*You, loving God, teach us to love the stranger; help
me do this and to be a person of kindness and service
to all in need.*

Having Godly Fun

> I know there is nothing better for them than to be
> happy and enjoy themselves as long as they live;
> moreover, it is God's gift that all should eat and
> drink and take pleasure in all their toil.
>
> (Ecclesiastes 3:12–13)

A cartoon shows a character looking at a sign as he gets ready to go onto a beach. The sign says, "No pets, no coolers, no swimming, no playing. . . . Have fun." As we read parts of the Bible, we may incorrectly assume that we aren't allowed to have any fun. The truth is that God does want us to enjoy ourselves and to be happy. As we pursue happiness, however, it is important to choose activities that will lead to true happiness and joy and will reflect our faithfulness to God. It can be helpful to ask, Does this activity reinforce my desire to honor God?

God of happiness and fun, help me to know which activities are part of your plan and which take me away from you; may I always choose with you in mind.

God Restores

> Then the nations that are left all around you shall know that I, the Lord, have rebuilt the ruined places, and replanted that which was desolate; I, the Lord, have spoken, and I will do it.
>
> (Ezekiel 36:36)

Sometimes we feel as if our life is in ruins, and there is a feeling of hollowness inside us. Sometimes we feel this way because we have not been at our best and other times it is because something bad has happened. Whether this hollow feeling is a result of our own actions or outside forces, we can look to God for help. Ezekiel's words helped those in exile after the defeat of their nation to know that God would help them. We too can take these words to heart and know that with God's help we can restore the "ruined places" in our life.

I turn to you, God, to help restore my spirit and fill the hollowness inside me.

What Type of Love?

"This is my commandment, that you love one another as I have loved you."

(John 15:12)

We say, "I love hamburgers," "I love my dog," or "I love my best friend." The word *love* takes a different meaning for each statement. Because we use the word *love* so casually and in so many different ways, we might misunderstand Jesus' commandment to love one another. This love that Jesus speaks of calls us to care deeply for the welfare of others. When we understand this, we understand the difficulty that can be involved in living this command. What about those classmates that we don't see eye to eye with, or the teacher that seems to give us a hard time, or the family member who is a constant source of struggle? Loving one another is a commandment that requires hard work.

God of love, help me to use the word love *correctly and to love others regardless of how difficult that may be.*

Honest Struggle

> The joy of our hearts has ceased; our dancing has been turned to mourning.
>
> (Lamentations 5:15)

When we suffer, our heart can't be joyful and it is hard to have fun. Instead of wanting to enjoy our friends or participate in our favorite activities, we might be morose or want to mope. As we struggle, we may find ourselves turning to God with our cares and concerns. The poem songs of the Book of Lamentations were written as an honest expression of the Israelites' deep struggles. These words summarize the universal feelings we all experience while suffering. The good news is that God is present in our sufferings. As we go through these hard times, we can ask, Am I am struggling with something that I want to bring to God? By sharing our suffering with God, we honestly admit we need help.

I can't laugh and play when I feel so bad, God. Help me to handle this struggle so I can return to the joy of life in you.

Popular and Wise

> People came from all the nations to hear the
> wisdom of Solomon; they came from all the kings
> of the earth who had heard of his wisdom.
>
> (1 Kings 4:34)

We don't often see the smartest kid in school being the
most popular. What if popularity came from being smart
or even wise? Wisdom is related to intelligence, but it
also encompasses insight and good judgment. Could the
wisest person be on the cover of magazines and have
groupies? If we valued wisdom like the people who came
to Solomon did, it could happen. If we respect people who
are wise, rather than flock to people just because we hear
they are popular, we'll honor a more godly perspective.
So the next time we're trying to be like someone, we can
ask, Would I gain more from being like the wise people
in my life rather than the popular ones?

*God, who doesn't distinguish popular from unpopular,
help me to respect those who are wise and follow the
people who will help me to honor you.*

God, Breath of Life

> Then the Lord God formed man from the dust
> of the ground, and breathed into his nostrils the
> breath of life; and the man became a living being.
>
> (Genesis 2:7)

Long before we take a science class, we realize how important breathing is. As a child, we might have tried to hold our breath and found out that we need air. Or we might have suffered, or witnessed, an asthma attack and realized that breathing is critical. In science we learn why oxygen, water, and nutrients are vital elements. We can live a few days without water and longer without food, but we can live without oxygen for only a few minutes. The image of the breath of life is one of the first images of God in the Bible. God is like oxygen, making it possible for us to live. The next time we take a breath, we can focus on that breath and pray in gratitude.

God, breath of life, as I breathe in, may I feel your presence and honor your name.

Joshua's Call

> "My servant Moses is dead. Now proceed to cross the Jordan, you and all these people, into the land that I am giving to them, to the Israelites."
>
> (Joshua 1:2)

When we take on a role that was filled successfully by a classmate, band mate, teammate, or other person, we say there are big shoes to fill. The person who held the position before us might have had the best SAT score, played her or his instrument perfectly, or scored the winning point in last year's game. As we step into those big shoes, we might feel nervous. When we stop worrying about that person and start doing what we are called to do, we begin to create our own legacy. We are each called to do something special and to have our own place. Joshua took over after Moses; he knew the sandals he was filling were very big. He did what God asked and enjoyed his own place in our faith's history.

God, as I learn to make my own way, help me to learn from Joshua and the others who have answered your call.

Pursue Justice

> If you pursue justice, you will attain it and wear it like a glorious robe.
>
> (Sirach 27:8)

To pursue something means to track it, chase after it, and practice it. Tracking something implies we want to learn its habits and ways. Chasing something implies we are willing to expend effort in following it. Practicing implies we commit to learning something and then keep doing it until we are good at it. If we pursue a sport or music, we can perform or compete in front of others with confidence. If we pursue justice, we will have to learn about it, chase after it, and practice it until we model it for others. Where do you see a need for justice? How can you respond, and who can help you?

Just and loving God, help me to track, chase after, and practice justice until I can model it for others.

Happy, Healthy Earth

> The wilderness and the dry land shall be glad,
>> the desert shall rejoice and blossom;
> like the crocus, it shall blossom abundantly,
>> and rejoice with joy and singing.
>
> (Isaiah 35:1–2)

Some of us live in cities or suburbs where we have limited contact with wilderness and land. In biblical times, the earth was interconnected with all aspects of life: people raised livestock, cultivated crops, and drew water from wells and springs. As they struggled through ordeals, oppression, and persecution, their flocks and lands suffered too by being destroyed or taken by force. As we read from Isaiah, when the Israelites returned from the Exile, it was as if the earth responded with great joy. How might your life and actions be cause for nature to respond in joy? What can you do to nurture your own direct relationship to the earth?

God, help me to live in a way that benefits all of your creation.

I Am Not

> "I am not the Messiah." And they asked [John the
> Baptist], "What then? Are you Elijah?" He said,
> "I am not. "Are you the prophet?" He answered,
> "No."
>
> (John 1:20–21)

Sometimes it is easier to know who we are not rather than who we are. As young people, we start to realize that we may not be a rock star, a professional athlete, or a movie actor, but we long to know what we are to be. As we try explore our different gifts and the different ways we might use them, we learn what we are good at and come closer to understanding what God calls us to be. It's important to know who we are *not* as well as who we *are*. What are some of your gifts and talents? What kinds of hobbies, jobs, or roles might these gifts and talents lead you to? Do these point to areas of interest you have? What might God be calling you to?

God, I long to know who I am and what you call me to be and do in this world. As I learn who I am not, let me be able to use that knowledge to better know who I am and what I may be.

Gaining Confidence

> I myself feel confident about you, my brothers and
> sisters, that you yourselves are full of goodness,
> filled with all knowledge, and able to instruct one
> another.

> (Romans 15:14)

When someone else has confidence in us, we develop self-esteem and may feel an obligation to live up to that confidence. As parents give us more responsibility, they are telling us that they are confident that we can live up to their expectations. As teachers give us harder assignments, they might be doing so because they feel we can handle more complex work. As we strive to follow Jesus more closely, we might want to know that we are living up to our responsibility as Christians. One way to know is to consider these questions: In what ways am I living up to the confidence Jesus has in me? How can I do a better job?

Christ, I want you to have the upmost confidence in me as your follower; guide me in the ways to achieve that.

Integrity and Acceptance

> All who hate me whisper together about me;
> they imagine the worst for me.
>
> (Psalm 41:7)

When people whisper behind our back, we want to do something to stop it or to make them accept us. We might even be tempted to do something that goes against our own values in order to be accepted. If we give up our integrity for the sake of acceptance, we run the risk of becoming like those who dislike us. We are called to a standard of integrity that is hard sometimes, especially if it results in our feeling unaccepted by our peers. Scripture reminds us, however, that God is steadfast in his acceptance of us. God is the one who upholds us when we maintain our integrity, which is a much better end result than being accepted by those who dislike us.

As I maintain my integrity in spite of those who don't like me, I pray that you, my Lord, uphold me and keep me in your presence forever.

Two Are Better Than One

Two are better than one, because they have a good reward for their toil.

(Ecclesiastes 4:9)

It is good to be alone sometimes; however, we cannot do certain things alone and without the help of others. It is important for us to have good friends and people who can help us with specific areas or tasks in our life. Those people who make our life easier by helping us are the type of friends we read about in Ecclesiastes. Getting help is not a sign of weakness or a lack of intelligence. It is actually a sign of maturity. Who are the friends in your life that help and support you? How can you be a helping friend to others?

God, who provides friends to help us as we go through life, may I be the type of friend who helps others, and may I choose friends who do the same for me.

Whom Do I Want to Be Like?

> Do not envy the wicked,
>   nor desire to be with them;
> for their minds devise violence,
>   and their lips talk of mischief.
>
> (Proverbs 24:1–2)

Not all peer pressure is bad. It's good when it motivates us to choose constructive activities, spend time with positive people, and improve ourselves. But some peer pressure is bad and can be especially bad if it encourages us to be like others who are not following God's ways. If we envy those people and want to be with them, we may pick up their traits. If they are disrespectful or violent, it may be easier for us to be that way too. As we choose friends, we can ask questions like, Are these the type of people who will help me to be my best, or are they the kind that may have a negative influence on me?

God, who only wants the best for me, help me to do my part by surrounding myself with friends who inspire me to greatness.

Parents First?

> For the Lord honors a father above his children,
> and he confirms a mother's right over her
> children.
>
> (Sirach 3:2)

We sometimes find it hard to honor and respect our parents. As we get older, we want to see ourselves as equal to our parents, but we know that our parents deserve a special respect. Although some parents abuse or neglect their children and act in ways that don't honor their own role and responsibility, most of us are in the situation where our parents are doing their best and deserve our full respect. How do you show honor and respect for your parents? Do you honor and respect your parents even when you might disagree with them about something?

Let me remember my respect for you, God, as I remember to respect my parents.

Holy and Acceptable

> I appeal to you therefore, brothers and sisters, by
> the mercies of God, to present your bodies as
> a living sacrifice, holy and acceptable to God,
> which is your spiritual worship.
>
> (Romans 12:1)

If we want to be holy and acceptable to God, we need to make decisions that support that intention. As we make decisions regarding sexual activity, thinking about presenting ourselves to God can be helpful. We may want time alone with the person we're attracted to, but being off by ourselves provides an opportunity to do things we wouldn't do if we were with others. As we are deciding how to express our care and concern with those we are forming deeper relationships with, we benefit from recalling the image of presenting ourselves to God.

As I think of being in front of you, I want to have a body that is holy and acceptable. I ask for your help, God, in making decisions that are good for me and pleasing to you.

Gracious Speech

> Let your speech always be gracious, seasoned
> with salt, so that you may know how you ought to
> answer everyone.

> (Colossians 4:6)

Our speech can convey many attitudes or emotions. When we compliment others or affirm them in some way, our speech is a source of joy. When we belittle or express prejudice or hatred, our words are a source of humiliation. If our words humiliate others or intimidate them, we are bullies. Before expressing our thoughts or emotions through speech, we should ask ourselves, Are the words I'm about to say courteous, considerate, and gracious? If we cannot answer yes to this question, then we should not say them.

May my words be kind, may I never use them to bully, and may I always be a reflection of you, loving God, in my speech.

The Beloved of the Lord

> Of Benjamin he said:
>   The beloved of the Lord rests in safety—
>   the High God surrounds him all day long—
>   the beloved rests between his shoulders.
>
> (Deuteronomy 33:12)

Some of us had favorite blankets or stuffed animals when we were little. These items helped us to feel secure. At some point we gave up those items (or at least put them out of sight). As we face issues or situations that make us feel insecure, it helps to have words to remember as a "security blanket." One such phrase could be from Deuteronomy, "The beloved of the Lord rests in safety" (33:12). When we are able to say those words in times of insecurity, we remember that we can rest our heads and our worries on the Lord's shoulders. Practicing the phrase now will make it easier to say when we are feeling anxious.

Lord, I rest my head on your shoulders and place my anxiety and worries in your care.

Tears to Action

> Cry aloud to the Lord!
>   O wall of daughter Zion!
> Let tears stream down like a torrent
>   day and night!
>
>   (Lamentations 2:18)

It is normal to cry out when we see or hear destruction. Watching the news can be overwhelming to us. When we feel sad because of the violence in our world, we may even shed tears. Our early ancestors of faith, when faced with the violent destruction of Jerusalem, also experienced strong emotions, and in Lamentations we hear some of their cries to God. The Israelites learned that they had to take specific actions to move out of their despair. When we ask ourselves, What do I need to do to respond to this type of violence? we start to move from tears and cries to action and healing.

Hear my prayers, Lord, and let the violence around me be calmed.

Really, This Is Life!

> They are to do good, to be rich in good works,
> generous, and ready to share, thus storing up for
> themselves the treasure of a good foundation for
> the future, so they may take hold of the life that
> really is life.
>
> (1 Timothy 6:18–19)

The society we live in often places great value on the accumulation of money or on the amount of material things a person has. As Catholics, our deepest values come from Scripture and Tradition. The First Letter to Timothy reminds us to place a higher value on who we are than on what we own. As we take a look at what we value, we need to ask ourselves: Is this important because society says it is, or because it helps me to do good works and be generous? Does it help me to "take hold of the life that really is life"?

Life in you, Christ, is the life that really is. May I place value on those things that are meaningful because of my faith rather than because of what society may say.

Do Not Covet Another Relationship

You shall not covet.

(Exodus 20:17)

When we are in a relationship, we might look at others' relationships and think that we want what they have. Maybe another couple seems to have more fun, more dates, or expresses more care and concern. We might even be attracted to a person who is part of that couple and feel tempted to break up the couple to gain what they have. If we covet a relationship or a person, we are breaking one of the Ten Commandments. When we covet another couple's relationship, we need to take a serious look at our own relationship first. Perhaps what we admire about another couple's relationship is the key to strengthening our own.

Lord, dating can be complicated. Help me to know what a good, healthy relationship is and to work on my own relationship rather than covet another's.

Courageous Faith

> O God, whose might is over all, hear the voice
> of the despairing, and save us from the hands of
> evildoers. And save me from my fear!
>
> (Esther 14:19)

As we are faced with doubt, our faith tradition's rich stories are a comfort. Hearing stories of others who felt doubt and who accomplished what they needed to do fills us with faith. Esther's story is one we can carry with us as we face the doubts that come with a faith-filled life. Her story tells how she courageously spoke up for her people and saved them from destruction. We each have a role to play in God's plan for his people. What doubts do you need to face so you can serve God as Esther did?

May I, when faced with doubt, be reminded of Esther and the others in our faith tradition who succeeded in what you, my God, called them to do.

Whom Am I Serving?

"No one can serve two masters; for a slave will either hate the one and love the other, or be devoted to the one and despise the other. You cannot serve God and wealth."

(Matthew 6:24)

We need a certain amount of material things in order to survive. We need food and clothes and housing and items that can assist us in school. But we often want unhealthy foods, the latest fashion in clothes, our own room, and the costliest laptop. Needing and wanting things are very different. When we want more stuff than we need or can afford, we start to serve wealth over God. We may even act in ungodly ways to get the things we want and ignore God's call to be generous with our money and belongings. As we assess what we need, we can start by asking, What is it that I truly *need*?

God, you are the only one I want to serve, help me not to be greedy but to be satisfied when my needs are met.

Words of Knowledge

> Cease straying, my child, from the words of
> knowledge, in order that you may hear instruction.
>
> (Proverbs 19:27)

Words of knowledge appear in many places. They might be in a textbook, in a teacher's lecture, or in a coach's advice. We might be able to get by without completing all the required reading. We might be able to pass a test without listening in class. We might be able to play a sport without acquiring new skills. However, when we only do part of the work required, we cheat ourselves and stray from the words of knowledge that bring us to better understanding. When we complete the reading, we begin to see the message between the lines. When we really listen to our teachers, we fully understand the concepts. When we do as our coaches suggest, we are more likely to improve our skills.

Keep me from straying from knowledge so that I may hear instruction, as well as your voice, O Lord.

Anger among Siblings

"But I say to you that if you are angry with a
brother or sister, you will be liable to judgment."

(Matthew 5:22)

Those of us with siblings are given an opportunity to have lifelong relationships. These relationships are filled with love and, at times, anger. The way we handle anger toward our siblings is critical to this lifelong relationship. Our parents may intervene, but we alone are responsible for our actions. When Jesus mentions a brother or sister, he may have meant anyone in our community, but his words apply to our actual siblings as well. If we are angry and do not work toward a resolution, we are liable to judgment. Therefore, we should ask ourselves: Is my anger unjustified or overblown? Am I intentionally feeding my anger? If the answer is yes to either question, we must work toward reconciliation.

Jesus Christ, my brother, I know you will always forgive me. May I also forgive my brothers and sisters when I am angry with them.

Committed to Loving One Another

Everyone who believes that Jesus is the Christ has been born of God, and everyone who loves the parent loves the child. By this we know that we love the children of God, when we love God and obey his commandments.

(1 John 5:1–2)

Commitments bind us to others. When we make a commitment, we know that we need to do our part to honor it and believe the other person will do the same. God's commitment to us is to care for us as an Eternal Father. Our commitment to God is to follow the Commandments, including the commandment Jesus gave to love one another. When we find it hard to love others, we can remember that we are fulfilling our commitment to God. If we love God, we must love the children of God. Before we act, we can ask ourselves, Is this how I'd treat a child of God? We fulfill our commitment to God when we can answer yes.

Help me to see all people as your children and to love them as you love us, our God.

Do Not Fear

Do not fear, for I am with you,
   do not be afraid for I am your God;
I will strengthen you, I will help you,
   I will uphold you with my victorious right
      hand.

(Isaiah 41:10)

In rain or bad weather, we look around for something to shield us from the elements. As we face a fearful situation, we hope for a shield of some sort to protect us. Sometimes it is hard to find the safe place. It is never hard, however, to find God. As Isaiah reminds us, the right hand of God is there for us as a shield when we are afraid. God promises to lend his strength and his help. Perhaps the next time we are fearful that God is not with us, we can raise our right hand up toward the victorious hand stretched out to uphold us.

I raise my hands to you, God, as I trust in your victorious right hand.

Christian Youth

> Let no one despise your youth, but set the believers
> an example in speech and conduct, in love, in
> faith, in purity.
>
> (1 Timothy 4:12)

Youthful followers of Christ often need to take words meant for adults and "translate" them into our own "language" and life circumstances. We may read Scripture stories and wonder, What do these stories mean for me, a Christian teenager? The First Letter to Timothy gives us a chance to hear what God called an early Christian youth to do. We can see what it means to be a Christian young person. In this case, we do not have to translate or try to interpret the meaning for us. We just need to be the examples of faith that Scripture calls us to be.

Timothy received straightforward instruction, and I pray to you, Lord Jesus, that I too can be an example to others as a Christian youth.

Facing God

> Yet even now, says the Lord,
>   return to me with all your heart,
> with fasting, with weeping, and with mourning.

> (Joel 2:12)

We are often ashamed to face a person we've wronged or to face those who have witnessed behavior we are not proud of. Once we face the person or face those who saw our actions, we are able to start on the path to forgiveness and reconciliation. We can apologize, and we can change our ways. In the same manner, we might turn away from God when we sin or are ashamed of our actions, but God never leaves us. God waits for us to return to him with all our heart. We can show God that we are sorry, and we can change our ways. By asking ourselves, In what ways have I turned away from God? we can get ready to return to the Lord.

Help me return to you, forgiving God, so that I can face you proudly.

Overcoming Evil

> Do not be overcome by evil, but overcome evil
> with good.
>
> (Romans 12:21)

A person of service and justice helps overcome evil with good. Service fights the evils of the world. Even if the service we are doing does not appear to overcome evil with good, most well-planned service opportunities help us to learn the complexities of poverty, homelessness, and other issues of justice. These complexities include politics, economics, business, and culture. They also include the need for human intervention, interaction, and concern. By doing good, interacting, helping, and caring, we start to unravel the complexities and are better able to overcome evil with good.

I want to do your will and be a person of service and justice, Lord, so that evil may be overcome with good.

Prayer to Gain Happiness

> Rejoice always, pray without ceasing, give thanks in all circumstances; for this is the will of God in Christ Jesus for you.
>
> (1 Thessalonians 5:16–18)

We notice that it is easy to start complaining if others are complaining or get frustrated or mad if others are expressing these emotions. It's also easy to stay in the mode of anger, frustration, or grievance once we are in that mind-set. As we hear the writer's advice in the First Letter to the Thessalonians, we are called, instead, to rejoice and pray and give thanks for all things. To do this, we must then surround ourselves with people who are positive, who have an active prayer life, and who are grateful and see the good in many different situations. When we surround ourselves with these people, it is easier for us to stay in the same mind-set. Even in times when we are justified in our anger or frustration, it may be beneficial to ask ourselves: What good can I find in this situation? Can I be prayerful and positive in order to change my mind-set?

I pray now and will try to make all I do a prayer to honor you, O God.

Peace and Hope

> Now may the Lord of peace himself give you
> peace at all times in all ways. The Lord be with all
> of you.

> (2 Thessalonians 3:16)

Times of great peace are rare. In our noisy, busy world,
we often have to intentionally look for peace and quiet.
We may find peace in nature, in church, or in our own
room. We may feel deep peace when we are on retreat
or when we spend time with good friends. A sense of
peace leads to a feeling of great hope, especially when
we feel confident that God is with us. If we draw on the
knowledge of God's presence, we gain peace in difficult
situations. And drawing on this peace, we find more
hope.

*God of peace and hope, may I be reminded of your
presence, and may that lead me to more times of
peace and hope.*

Love of Neighbor

> Love does no wrong to a neighbor; therefore, love
> is the fulfilling of the law.
>
> (Romans 13:10)

When we think of love, we usually think of it either in terms of romance or family. Doing no wrong in those relationships sounds logical. If we think of love only as a close emotional connection, then doing no wrong to our neighbor may not seem to have any connection to love. Paul reminds us that love fulfills God's Law. He challenges us to realize that love is not just romantic or family based, but neighborly as well. Paul used the term *neighbor* to mean everyone we encounter, including those who live nearby. Who would you consider to be your neighbors, and what can you do to include them in your circle of love and care?

As I learn to love, let be mindful of those whom I call neighbor. Help me to be respectful and caring toward them as a reflection of your love and Law, O God.

Strength through Suffering

> "And so observe, from generation to generation, that none of those who put their trust in him will lack strength."

> (1 Maccabees 2:61)

We suffer in big and little ways. Physical and emotional pain makes us suffer, especially if it is long term. Family situations, such as fighting, divorce, or distance make us suffer. We suffer through pains like a failing friendship or a crush that is unrequited. The Israelites suffered under Greek occupation, and the forces known as the Maccabees led the Jews in a successful revolt by placing their trust in God. Whether we are suffering through a crisis or a minor annoyance, we can ask ourselves, How can I remember to maintain my own strength by placing my trust in God?

May the strength you provide, protector God, help me through all my sufferings, great and small.

Real Popularity

> For I am the least of the apostles, unfit to be called an apostle, because I persecuted the church of God.

> (1 Corinthians 15:9)

Paul's popularity grew after he became a follower of Christ and changed his ways. His conversion turned him from a persecutor of Christians to one of the most influential early missionaries. His words and legacy are contained in many of the letters of the New Testament in the Bible, the best-selling book in history. If we try to be popular for the wrong reasons, we may succeed for a short time but certainly not in the long run. At first, we may gain the false respect and attention that we seek. As time goes on, our admirers usually find the next "great thing" and go on to make another person popular. If, however, our popularity comes from others' respect for our values, the example we set, and the good things we do, it is a popularity that comes naturally and is rooted in something that is longer lasting.

Lord, help me to let go of any need I might have to be popular and, instead, to focus first on being the best person I can be.

Light of Life

> Again Jesus spoke to them, saying, "I am the light of the world. Whoever follows me will never walk in darkness but will have the light of life."
>
> (John 8:12)

Darkness can be scary, uncomfortable, and dangerous. Most of us like to have streetlights as we walk home at night or as we cross a parking lot. When we camp, we keep a flashlight nearby. When we were little children, we may have needed a night-light to feel safe. We have electricity, batteries, and generators to make as much light available as we need. In Jesus' time, light came from an oil lamp, a torch, or a fire. The people of his time were limited in their activities because they had to rely on these less efficient light sources. Saying that Jesus was the light of life had a strong impact on his early followers. As we listen to those words, we can ask ourselves, Where do I need to shed some light—in my own life and for others?

Light of the World, you provide that light for me. May I be light for others as well.

Simon and Andrew

> And Jesus said to them, "Follow me and I will make you fish for people." And immediately they left their nets and followed him.
>
> (Mark 1:17–18)

We are busy people with lives filled with school, extracurricular activities, work, family, and friends. Most of us are not fishing, but we may be studying, surfing the Web, taking part in school activities, working, or just spending time with our friends. Often we are so busy that we do not stop and listen to God's voice. It's there, calling to us, but we're busy and might miss it. Andrew and Simon were busy fishing when Jesus called them, but they stopped what they were doing immediately to follow him. How often do you take time to really listen for God's voice in your life?

I am so busy that I may not hear you, God. Help me to settle my heart and listen for your call.

Create Justice

> As you have done, it shall be done to you; your deeds shall return on your own head.
>
> (Obadiah 1:15)

What goes around comes around. Have you ever heard that saying? Isn't that exactly what Obadiah is saying is verse 15? Whatever you do comes back to you eventually. Does this mean that if we give someone a dollar, we will get a dollar back? It may not, but it can indicate that by being charitable, we are creating a world in which charity and care come that much closer to being the norm. And we and future generations benefit from that! We can be actively involved in creating the world we want to live in. So, although we shouldn't do things only for our own benefit, we know that by doing our part to make the world a better place, we are creating a world in which we, ourselves, will be happier to live in.

God of all fairness, help me to do my part to create a just place here on earth.

Holding the Earth Together

> He himself is before all things, and in him all
> things hold together.
>
> (Colossians 1:17)

We look at a river, lake, or ocean and see so much water
that we think it will last forever. We see store shelves
filled with bread, fruits, and vegetables and think there
is plenty for all. Because we have so much, we may not
see the need to protect the earth, thinking it will just keep
producing for us. But the earth needs to be held together,
and that is what Jesus Christ does. He sustains all things,
and we can help with that work. In order for our children
and our children's children to have stores full of healthy
items from the earth, we need to take care of it now. We
can start by asking ourselves, Is what I am doing helping
to hold the earth together, or am I tearing the earth apart?

*I promise, Jesus, sustainer of all things, to help hold
the earth together by protecting and caring for it.*

Loyal Child in the Faith

> To Timothy, my loyal child in the faith: Grace, mercy, and peace from God the Father and Christ Jesus our Lord.
>
> (1 Timothy 1:2)

Some of us may call our friends' parents "Mom" or "Dad" because they treat us like their own children. This loving extension of the family circle feels good and is actually a helpful asset for our development. The author of this letter called Timothy a loyal child in the faith because he felt both fatherly toward him and connected in faith. We too are connected to others in our faith. We learn how to live as Christians from our own parents, our friends' parents, and our family of faith. We can ask, How can I behave so that others might call me a loyal child in the faith?

As your child, Lord, may I be called loyal, and may I be filled with your grace, mercy, and peace.

Different Gifts

> We have gifts that differ according to the grace given to us: prophecy, in proportion to faith; ministry, in ministering; the teacher, in teaching; the exhorter, in exhortation; the giver, in generosity; the leader, in diligence; the compassionate, in cheerfulness.
>
> (Romans 12:6–8)

God blesses each of us with unique gifts. We may not be good at everything, but each of us has been blessed with some special talents. Because of this, we are responsible for developing our God-given gifts to our best ability. The Letter to the Romans encourages us to recognize and use our "gifts that differ." In this way, we can celebrate the meeting of God's creativity with our own uniqueness. When we use our gifts for the good of all, we contribute to the entire Body of Christ throughout the world.

Thank you, Lord Jesus, for my own particular gifts and talents. Help me to remember that when I share them with others I bring your love to the world.

Always Accepted

> Happy are those who live in your house,
>> ever singing your praise.

> (Psalm 84:4)

As we walk through life, it can sometimes seem like every door is closed to us. We may see possibilities but find no way to make them a reality. Will we ever find a place and a purpose? There is one place, however, where we are always welcome, always accepted, always at home. God's house, our parish church, accepts us no matter what our grade point average, singing ability, popularity, or athletic prowess. If we want a place to belong, our parish church has wide open doors. If it doesn't feel that way to us right now, we can ask ourselves, Where do I belong in my parish? and then seek out a pastor, religious education director, or youth minister to guide us.

God, when I long to be accepted, help me to walk through the open doors of your love in my parish church. Help me to find my place in my parish where I can sing your praise and join others in loving service!

A Faithful Friend

> "Where you go, I will go;
>   where you lodge, I will lodge;
> your people shall be my people,
>   and your God my God."
>
> (Ruth 1:16)

Close friends want to spend time together. We may stay overnight at each other's houses, sign up for the same classes, and even make college plans together. In friendship, differences—even of race or culture—are respected and celebrated. A woman named Ruth, in the Old Testament, was a Gentile. Yet she was faithful to Naomi, her mother-in-law and friend, who was a Jew. Ruth's experience helps us to understand that God's plan of salvation is for all people. As a Gentile, Ruth was considered an outsider. But as we learn later, she became King David's great-grandmother and an ancestor of Jesus Christ. When we ask ourselves, Am I a faithful friend? we can look to Ruth for encouragement and example.

God of all people, help me to respect and celebrate differences and to be willing to open the gift of my friendship to all.

Independence Day

> I shall walk at liberty, for I have sought your
> precepts.
>
> (Psalm 119:45)

We are blessed to live in a country in which religious freedom is preserved and valued. We know that freedom is something we can't take for granted, and is accompanied by responsibility. As citizens we have the responsibility to live in a way that builds up our communities and our country. As Christians we have the responsibility to live as faith-filled people. As we celebrate our independence as a nation, we can celebrate our freedom to worship as Christians, and to support the rights of others to follow their own conscience in their worship of God. Before we light fireworks and eat cherry pie, we can start the celebration by asking ourselves, How do I show my appreciation for the freedom I have?

Thank you, God, for the freedom of worship we enjoy in the United States of America. Help me to live my thanks with an attitude of respect toward the religious choices of others.

Building Up

> What should be done then, my friends? When you come together, each one has a hymn, a lesson, a revelation, a tongue, or an interpretation. Let all things be done for building up.
>
> (1 Corinthians 14:26)

When we gather for Mass, we come together as Catholic peers, and it sometimes takes a little "positive pressure" from each of us to help one another in praying together. If we participate by singing or reciting prayers, those around us are more likely to do the same. The simple decision of choosing to sit where we can best participate (perhaps near the front instead of the back) can make a difference in our attitude. So before we choose a place in church next Sunday, we first may want to ask ourselves, Will I help build up the Church with my active participation, or will I distract myself and others from attention to God in prayer?

Lord Jesus, you gave your life that we might live. Help me to find ways to honor your death and celebrate your risen life within me as I participate in our Sunday Mass each week.

Be Kind to Your Parents

A child who gathers in summer is prudent,
but a child who slumbers during harvest
brings shame.

(Proverbs 10:5)

In earlier, agrarian times, the family unit was also the family business. At certain times of the year, especially during spring planting and fall harvesting, all hands were needed to get the job done. A son or daughter who refused to contribute to the family labor would certainly be a disgrace, especially if that son or daughter expected to benefit from the proceeds! Things are different now, but parents still have a right to expect cooperation from all family members, especially in times of stress or other need. Your parents' desires may not be your preference, but if all hands are needed to accomplish something as a family, be kind and considerate. Step up. Help keep the "family business" afloat. Be a credit!

God, our Father, show me ways to be a credit to my family through kindness and consideration.

Words of Respect

> Entirely out of place is obscene, silly, and vulgar talk; but instead, let there be thanksgiving.
>
> (Ephesians 5:4)

There are times and places for talking about sex, and these times and places are with those who truly love us and are concerned for our welfare. When we keep talk about sexuality and relationships at a respectful level, we reveal our inner attitude toward ourselves and others: gratitude for God's gift to us in making us who we are as sexual beings and bearers of his gift of life. This attitude toward sexuality is truly countercultural: People are not objects to be used and then discarded. We can take a stand for dignity, privacy, and respect by steering clear of inappropriate sexual references in our speech. All vulgar and crude talk is beneath our dignity as human beings and as followers of Christ, who are called to show respect for all.

Thank you, God, for the gift of my sexuality; help me to show my gratitude by respecting myself and others in my words and actions.

You're Different

> You shall not wrong or oppress a resident alien,
> for you were aliens in the land of Egypt.
>
> (Exodus 22:21)

Many of us won't bully someone in person; it is hard to say or do things face-to-face. However, some of us may think we can write things in a text, blog, or Web site because, through the marvels of technology, we can remain anonymous. Often the first person to be targeted is the one seen as different, new, or foreign to us. Even if we mean no harm, drawing attention to someone else's characteristics, especially if we see them as negative, can be cruel, and also highlights a certain immaturity and narrow-mindedness on our part. As a direct slam or an indirect critique, we are showing disrespect to another human being that God created. We need to ask ourselves, before blogging or texting, Would I want this written about me?

Thank you, God, for making each of us unique and different. Help me to see the positive in myself and in others.

The Lord Is Confidence

Do not be afraid of sudden panic,
   or of the storm that strikes the wicked;
for the Lord will be your confidence
   and will keep your foot from being caught.

(Proverbs 3:25–26)

Fear can paralyze us. Fear can negate free choice. Fear of the opinion of others, for example, can lead us to do things we wouldn't normally do. Yet fear is useful because it serves as a warning to us of an unsafe situation, or one that we are not fully prepared to handle. In such cases, fear is a helpful reaction. But irrational fears can hinder our development as human beings or our freedom as children of God. When this happens, turn to God. God loves us and wants us to be free from fear and anxiety. We can find wisdom and comfort in his living Word in Scripture. If we find ourselves locked in fear, we can say, The Lord is my confidence, and move forward into life.

Lord of confidence, I turn to you with all my fears and ask for your strength.

Violence and Peace

> The wolf shall live with the lamb,
>   the leopard shall lie down with the kid,
> the calf and the lion and the fatling together.

> (Isaiah 11:6)

Can we imagine a notorious bully sitting at lunch with the person he or she has always picked on? Can we imagine the most popular kids asking the least popular to the next dance? Can we imagine the person who scares us offering us a gesture of peace? If so, we can imagine the Prophet Isaiah's amazing prophecy regarding God's Reign. God wants his people to not only get along but also thrive and grow together. As young people we can work toward this reality in our own schools and communities. Teen violence takes many forms: bullying, verbal abuse, shunning, and physical violence. We can begin to work for peace by honestly answering, Where is the violence in my life? Then we can ask the further question, How can I be a channel of God's peace?

God of peace and justice, help me to work for peace and eliminate violence, whether near or far away.

Look Forward

> Jesus said to him, "No one who puts a hand to the plow and looks back is fit for the kingdom of God."
>
> (Luke 9:62)

If the farmer looks back while plowing a field, he will inadvertently make the row behind him crooked, which is exactly what he does not want to do. If we look straight ahead toward a goal, we are more likely to reach it. If we look backward to see how we are doing, we may lose sight of our objective. Jesus is saying, "Go for the goals of the Kingdom, and don't be too self-conscious about it!" Our faith is one of forward motion built on Scripture and the Tradition of the Church. We need to keep childish or even sinful things in the past where they belong. We need to ask forgiveness in the Sacrament of Penance and Reconciliation, and then move forward. How might you work toward more love and peace in your life?

God, help me to keep my hand on the plow and my eyes set on the goals of the Kingdom of peace and love.

The Presence of God

> For I am convinced that neither death, nor life, nor
> angels, nor rulers, nor things present, nor things
> to come, nor powers, nor height, nor depth,
> nor anything else in all creation, will be able to
> separate us from the love of God in Christ Jesus
> our Lord.
>
> (Romans 8:38–39)

Sometimes we need to put distance between ourselves
and temptation: people, places, and things that can lead
us down the wrong path. We can't, however, put distance
between ourselves and God's love. God is there as we
date, as we dance, and as we do all we do. That means
that we need to ask ourselves, Am I pretending that God is
not here? If we are trying to pretend that God isn't present
on our dates, we are probably dating the wrong people
or doing the wrong things.

*God, I invite you on my next date. Sit with me as I
sit with the person I'm dating, dance with us, and be
ever present as we live in your love.*

Asking in Faith

> But ask in faith, never doubting, for the one who doubts is like a wave of the sea, driven and tossed by the wind; for the doubter, being double-minded and unstable in every way, must not expect to receive anything from the Lord.

> (James 1:6)

Does asking in faith mean that we will always get what we ask for? In most people's experience, sometimes the answer to prayer is no. Does this mean that faith was lacking? Not necessarily. The question is, What do we have faith *in*? In the validity of our request? No. We have faith in God, and in God's loving wisdom. When we pray in faith, we always pray with the idea that our Father knows best. We know that we are not God. We cannot see around every corner. We pray with trust that God, in his infinite love for us, will give us exactly what we need, no matter what our prayer. God's love is our anchor in the stormy seas of doubt. Trust in his love will keep us afloat!

God, may your love be my anchor in times of doubt and distress.

Two Coins

> A poor widow came and put in two small copper
> coins, which are worth a penny. Then he called
> his disciples and said to them, "Truly I tell you, this
> poor widow has put in more than all those who
> are contributing to the treasury."
>
> (Mark 12:42–43)

Jesus concluded by saying that all of the others gave out of
abundance; the poor widow gave from all that she had.
According to Jesus, the call to generosity means giving
everything we have, giving with our whole heart. If the
ideal is "everything," can we at least attempt to give, out
of our time, talent, and treasure, something substantial?
The next time we are asked to give, we can ask ourselves:
Am I giving everything? Or at least something substantial?
Or am I giving just my *leftover* time, talent, or treasure?

*Jesus, you gave everything for us. May we share our
time, talent, and treasure with others wholeheartedly.*

Helpful Criticism

> It is better to hear the rebuke of the wise than to
> hear the song of fools.
>
> (Ecclesiastes 7:5)

A baseball coach once said to his team, "I don't want anyone getting upset with criticism. If I didn't think you could improve, I wouldn't bother with you." Yet criticism or "rebukes," are often hard to accept because they pierce our fragile egos and show us reality. But behind every rebuke or criticism is another reality: that of care, concern, and belief in the person we can become. The wise rebuke of a parent, teacher, or coach may not seem "better than a song," but it does help us to learn and grow. The proper response to every criticism is realizing that we will be the better for it and saying, "Thanks very much for pointing that out." Then we show our gratitude in our efforts at improvement. It is not easy, but it is worth it.

God of wisdom, may I accept the criticism of parents, teachers, and coaches with gratitude.

Jesus Is Angry

> Then Jesus entered the temple and drove out all
> who were selling and buying in the temple, and
> he overturned the tables of the money changers
> and the seats of those who sold doves.
>
> (Matthew 21:12)

We get to know all of Jesus through Scripture. We meet
him even before he is born and learn the stories of his
birth, of his childhood, and of his ministry. Jesus reveals
himself to us through his words and actions as recorded
in the Gospels. The most surprising account for some of us
is of that of Jesus showing anger. In this instance, we see
a side of Jesus we don't think about very often. We learn
that his anger is justifiable, and that anger is a very human
reaction in some situations. But like all human reactions, it
must be controlled. The next time we are angry, we can
ask ourselves, Is this anger justifiable?

*Jesus, may my controlled and justifiable anger
motivate me to change unjust situations, to defend
those weaker than me, and to seek your peace.*

Vows and Oaths

> When a man makes a vow to the Lord, or swears an oath to bind himself by a pledge, he shall not break his word; he shall do according to all that proceeds out of his mouth.
>
> (Numbers 30:2)

"I promise." What does this mean? In some cases, a promise is a small one and easy to keep: "I promise to call if I'm running late." Small promises are not unimportant; keeping smaller commitments prepares us for keeping bigger ones. The bigger promises that we make are sealed with an oath or a vow and are made in God's name: "So help me, God." An oath to tell the truth in court or a wedding vow are examples of these bigger promises. Keeping smaller promises now will help us to keep the bigger promises we swear to keep, under oath or vow, as adults. Now, before making even a small promise, we can ask ourselves, Is this a promise I intend to keep?

I pray to you, my God, that I do my best to keep my promises, especially ones I make in your name.

Rock and Refuge

On God rests my deliverance and my honor;
my mighty rock, my refuge is in God.

Trust in him at all times, O people;
pour out your heart before him;
God is a refuge for us.

(Psalm 62:7–8)

In nice weather, reading, writing, or painting outside can be pleasant. But when the wind starts to blow, we put rocks on our papers or other light objects to hold them down. If we don't, we run the risk of things blowing away. Our trust in God is a little like those papers and other light objects; without God the rock holding it down, all kinds of things—like fear and worry—can blow our trust away. Trusting in God means pouring out our heart in all truth and saying: I'm counting on you, God, to be my rock. Let's face this together. God, our rock, is the protection that holds firm.

God, my rock and my refuge, I surrender my fears and worries to you. Open my heart to a greater trust in you.

Learning Faith

> So then, brothers and sisters, stand firm and hold fast to the traditions that you were taught by us, either by word of mouth or by our letter.
>
> (2 Thessalonians 2:15)

We learn about our faith in different ways. We might participate in religious education classes or join in a youth ministry program. We might also learn from others who participate with us in faith-related activities, like liturgy, retreats, and service projects. Some of us like to read about our faith to understand it more fully. Most of us learn from the example of others, by watching what faith-filled people do. Faith-filled people know their faith, stand firm in it, and hold fast to Scripture and the Tradition of the Church as explained by the Pope and bishops. If we want to know more of what it means to be a Catholic, we can start by asking ourselves the question, Who are the people I can learn from and talk to about my faith?

God, may I learn what it means to be Catholic by seeking out others who follow you.

Fessing Up

> And the Israelites said to the Lord, "We have sinned; do to us whatever seems good to you; but deliver us this day!"
>
> (Judges 10:15)

When we do something wrong and "get away with it," we might not be punished in the usual ways, like being grounded or getting a bad grade. However, if we have a rightly formed conscience, we usually feel a healthy sense of guilt. Yet guilt is not easy to bear. We may realize that it is easier to confess, or "fess up" and seek forgiveness, than to continue to live with guilt. The Sacrament of Penance and Reconciliation can help us, even if our lapse is not a mortal sin and we are not obliged to confess it. To restore a good relationship, it is helpful as well to admit our error personally. Doing something to make things right may be necessary. When we've done something wrong, the question, Why do I feel so bad about this? can lead us to act like the Israelites and fess up.

Help me, God, to seek forgiveness when I have wronged you and others.

Serving Jesus

> "And the king will answer them, 'Truly I tell you,
> just as you did it to one of the least of these who
> are members of my family, you did it to me.'"
>
> (Matthew 25:40)

Jesus tells his followers that we are going to be judged based on how well we feed, clothe, care for, and visit others. When do we have the opportunity to serve the Lord soup, to offer him a drink of water, or to put a coat on his back? When we serve Jesus in others, especially those in need. Yet we are all so busy! Sometimes we are asked to do service projects on a weekend that conflicts with another opportunity that sounds like much more fun. This conflict presents us with a choice. We need to have fun, but we do need to balance our fun with work and service. When making those choices, we can ask ourselves, What is Jesus asking me to do for him?

Jesus, who calls me to service, may I choose to serve you in all those who are members of your family.

True Happiness

> You show me the path of life.
>> In your presence there is fullness of joy;
>> in your right hand are pleasures forevermore.
>
> (Psalm 16:11)

We might find fleeting pleasure when we win a game or get a great grade. We enjoy spending times with friends and going out. But when the next game doesn't go in our favor or we don't do so well in a competition or we can't find a date for a special occasion, joy is nowhere to be found. We find that sometimes happiness is fleeting or only on the surface. We learn about true happiness when we follow God's path in life. Does following God's path mean we will never care about winning games, or getting good grades, or having friends? No, God wants us to be happy. But there is a deeper, more permanent joy in knowing that we are in God's hands. Happiness grows as we more closely follow him. Our little joys and disappointments teach us what true happiness means for us along our own particular path.

God, show me the path of life, and the way to true happiness.

Sure and Steadfast Hope

> We have this hope, a sure and steadfast anchor of the soul, a hope that enters the inner shrine behind the curtain, where Jesus, a forerunner on our behalf, has entered, having become a high priest forever according to the order of Melchizedek.
>
> (Hebrews 6:19–20)

In the Christian life, we sometimes have a "cross" or a trial to bear. These are part of life, but Jesus has gone before us and is with us now as an anchor of hope. If you have ever faced a dental visit or a trip to the principal's office, you know that having someone with you (like a parent or good friend), waiting for you, can provide you some comfort. Jesus is with us and always waiting for us; he is the comfort on the other end of any ordeal life hands us. The Letter to the Hebrews reminds us of this hope. No matter what we have to face in life, we find hope and comfort in Jesus.

Lord Jesus, be my anchor of hope in difficult times.

Love Aligned

> And this is my prayer, that your love may overflow more and more with knowledge and full insight to help you to determine what is best, so that in the day of Christ you may be pure and blameless, having produced the harvest of righteousness that comes through Jesus Christ for the glory and praise of God.
>
> (Philippians 1:9–10)

Some say that love makes us silly or giddy, dim-witted, or slow. This may be especially true for romantic love or sexual attraction. But love does change us. Love that is good and holy helps us to grow as human beings and leads us to a deeper relationship with God. The love that comes from God forms the best foundation of any relationship. It is marked by respect, caring, and joy. If you are able to say yes to questions like these: Does this relationship make me a better person? Does it bring me closer to God? then your love may well be aligned to Gospel values.

God of all love, help me to choose good relationships that strengthen my relationship with you and with those I love.

It's Not God's Fault

> In all this Job did not sin or charge God with
> wrongdoing.
>
> (Job 1:22)

It is easy to blame someone else when we are suffering.
We say: "That teacher gave me a bad grade," or "My
friend did this to me so I did that to him." We may be
tempted to say, "God is doing this to me!" when we
are suffering. Job suffered many setbacks; he lost family,
property, and friends. Yet Job never blamed God. Job's
patience is an example for us in our own sufferings. If our
suffering is our own doing (for example, we didn't study
for a test), we need to own up to it. Our pain teaches us to
make a different choice the next time. And if our suffering
is a result of our frail human existence (as the illness or
death of a loved one), we turn to God in faith and trust.
We thank him for sending us Jesus, who conquered pain
and death, and who, one day, will wipe all our tears
away.

*God, just and compassionate, in my times of suffering,
may I turn to you in faith and trust.*

Humble Popularity

> My child, perform your tasks with humility; then
> you will be loved by those whom God accepts.
>
> (Sirach 3:17)

The root of the word *humility* is *humus*, meaning earth.
Humble people are down-to-earth people, easy to talk to,
comfortable to be with. Some are even popular. Others
try to be popular by bragging about what they do. Can
someone be humble, popular, and talented? Of course.
The humble person recognizes that all gifts and talents
come from God, and are to be used in service of others.
Being humble doesn't mean we can't be proud of what
we do or accept praise. It just means that praise from
others is not our goal. Our goal is to be and do our very
best. The question, Am I doing my best at this with thanks
and praise to God? is the starting point for humility. If the
end result is popularity, accept it with humble gratitude!

*Help me to be humble, God, and to live my life for
your glory.*

Bread of Life

"I am the bread of life."

(John 6:35)

We know some things are essential for survival—air, water, food. Without air for more than a few minutes, without water for a few days, and without food for a few weeks, we perish. Of course, that is what we need for survival alone. We know that living is more than just survival. To live a full human life, we need more than air, water, and food. We need so many other intangibles—love, peace, friendship, joy. And we need Jesus. Jesus gives us life, not only for our bodies (for physical life also comes from God) but also for our spirits. In Jesus, the Bread of Life, we are united with him, the source of all life. We might say, "I can survive without Jesus," but can we say, "I can live without Jesus"? The only question is, when Jesus knocks at the door of our hearts, will we let him in?

Jesus, Bread of Life, may I open the door to you, the source of my true life.

Mary's Yes

> Then Mary said, "Here am I, the servant of the
> Lord; let it be with me according to your word."
> Then the angel departed from her.
>
> (Luke 1:38)

We might have fleeting moments or flashes of insight telling us to gravitate toward a certain vocation or career. We might know trusted adults who point us in certain directions. Some of us will meet priests or religious who tap us and say, "I think God is calling you too." But most of us won't have angels visiting, telling us what our calling is. Mary didn't expect to be visited by the angel. She must have been surprised and was probably afraid. Never could she have imagined such a vocation, such a call from God! Yet she answered with a yes that brought Jesus to her and to all of us. As we explore our own callings, we need to ask ourselves, Am I going to answer God's call with a yes, as Mary did?

God, who heard Mary say, "Let it be done to me,"
help me to hear the whispers of my calling and
answer yes to you as well.

Prince of Peace

And they shall live secure, for now he shall be
    great
  to the ends of the earth;
and he shall be the one of peace.

(Micah 5:4–5)

We look up to our leaders for direction. From our coaches, we find direction in athletics; from our advisers, we find direction in choosing classes and activities; and from our Church leaders, we find direction for our spiritual and moral well-being. All leaders teach us about leadership styles as well as about athletics, choices at school, or our Catholic faith. The Prophet Micah tells us of the type of leader the Messiah will be. What will the savior be like? Where will he lead us? The answer is in Jesus. Jesus comes to us as the Prince of Peace. Jesus is a peaceful and just leader and so, as his followers, we too are called to be peaceful and just. The question, How am I following Jesus' example of peace and justice? will help us to move in the direction he points.

Jesus, Prince of Peace, help me to move toward a more just and peaceful world, starting with me.

Earth as Art

> You cause the grass to grow for the cattle,
>   and plants for people to use,
> to bring forth food from the earth,
>   and wine to gladden the human heart,
> oil to make the face shine,
>   and bread to strengthen the human heart.
>
> (Psalm 104:14–15)

If we create a work of art and someone throws paint on it or crushes it, we become sad or even angry. If it was a piece of artwork for a class or a project, we may even suffer consequences in our grade point average. God created grass and grapes and wheat and water so that we have nourishment and food to enjoy. As humans we are called to care for all of God's creation. We need to care for it because God created it and because we rely on this earth to survive. As we go about our daily lives, we can ask ourselves, What one thing can I do today to help care for God's creation?

Creator of all good and wonderful things that we enjoy to eat and drink, may I help to care for the earth so that these things are available to us all.

You Are Perfect

> So God created humankind in his image,
>> in the image of God he created them;
>> male and female he created them.

> (Genesis 1:27)

In the Book of Genesis, we learn that God created the earth and sky, water and plants, animals and birds and called them "good." At the culminating point of creation, as the story tells us, God created the human being, not only good but in his own image. Does that mean we are perfect? Yes! Perfection does not mean matching an unrealistic "ideal" but rather being unique and true to ourselves. (Every tree is different, yet every tree is a perfect tree. It is the same with us.) Even our physical characteristics—crazy hair or big ears—are part of our own unique perfection. Think about this when you look in the mirror. God made you and loves you. You are unique and perfect, just the way you are.

God, the next time I look in the mirror, I will accept my own perfect uniqueness; help me to reflect all that you are to the world.

For Ourselves and Others

> Many Samaritans from that city believed in him
> because of the woman's testimony.
>
> (John 4:39)

When we are shunned by our peers, we know how the woman at the well felt. She fetched water when no one was around, probably because she was not accepted. After her encounter with Jesus, she told others about him. Jesus had given her a sense of peace and self-esteem that she did not feel until their conversation. Because of this woman's testimony, others came to believe in Jesus. Our own self-esteem can be greatly enhanced by remembering that Jesus comes to each of us just as he did the woman at the well. And if we share his word, we may be like the woman at the well, who brought others to believe in Christ.

Christ, please help me to believe in myself through my faith in you.

A Welcoming Spirit

> So if you consider me your partner, welcome him
> as you would welcome me.
>
> (Philemon 1:17)

It can be hard when a new person is introduced into our circle of friends by one of the group. Our first reaction may be to ignore or reject the new person. We may find it hard to accept someone when we haven't initiated the relationship. But any friend of our friend should be welcomed by us. Through such a spirit of openness and welcoming, we develop a group of people whom we can call friends and partners. We also treat others in the way we would want to be treated. Although accepting others may sometimes seem burdensome, the end result can be gratifying, and it glorifies God. The next time a friend brings along a "tag-along" friend, we can start the cycle of acceptance by asking ourselves, How can I be a welcoming person and learn or grow because of this new acquaintance?

Loving God, teach me to be welcoming to newcomers in my social circle and to all people I meet.

Drama or Harmony?

> May the God of steadfastness and encouragement grant you to live in harmony with one another, in accordance with Christ Jesus, so that together you may with one voice glorify the God and Father of our Lord Jesus Christ.
>
> (Romans 15:5–6)

Friends who stir up trouble and create drama can leave us feeling unsteady and emotionally exhausted. If this dynamic is common, then the relationship is probably an unhealthy one. Friends who create drama are often not the ones who are going to encourage us to live in harmony with others and in a loving relationship with God. As we work to develop healthy friendships, we can ask ourselves, Does this person help me to be a positive person who loves God and lives in harmony with others? It is important to surround ourselves with friends who support us in our faith and in building positive relationships, rather than friends who create conflict in our life.

Lord, help me to choose friends who are harmonious and who will help me to be faithful to you.

Influence to Do Good

> When he came and saw the grace of God, he rejoiced, and he exhorted them all to remain faithful to the Lord with steadfast devotion.
>
> (Acts of the Apostles 11:23–24)

In our relationships with friends and peers, we can influence one another in good ways or in bad ways. When others pressure us to do something that is not right, we choose whether to give in or to resist the pressure. In the same way, when someone pressures us to do something that is good, we can choose to rise to the challenge or to ignore it. Pressure to do something positive is an exhortation—a call to choose and do good. Like Paul, we should encourage others to choose what is good. We should also resist pressure from others to do what we know in our heart is wrong and displeasing to God. We can ask ourselves: How can I encourage others to do the right thing? How can I grow strong in resisting the pressure to do wrong?

Dear Lord, help me to always resist what displeases you. Guide me in leading others to you.

My Brother's Keeper

"Am I my brother's keeper?"

(Genesis 4:9)

It's not always easy to deal with our brothers and sisters. Sometimes having an older or younger sibling around is no fun at all. Some of us choose to handle this challenge by ignoring or shunning a sibling. Of course God wants us to love our brothers and sisters and all our family. Even when being kind and patient with family members is not easy, we should focus on how important our family is and remember that God blesses families and gives them strength to live in love and grow in faith together. The next time you feel like Cain, who said to God about his brother Abel, "Am I my brother's keeper?" ask yourself instead: Do my actions always show that I love my family? How can I do better?

God, thank you for my family. Strengthen our bond and our love, and bless us as we strive to show our care for one another.

Choosing Chastity

"For this is the will of God, your sanctification: that you abstain from fornication; that each one of you know how to control your own body in holiness and honor."

(1 Thessalonians 4:3–4)

At times we might feel pressure to engage in sexual acts even though we know that doing so is wrong. Sometimes the pressure is imposed by another person, sometimes we impose it on ourselves because we think we have to be sexually active to be accepted or to keep a relationship. It can be hard to exercise good judgment and be strong when faced with a choice regarding sexual activity. Always honor the holiness of your body and make choices that reflect that. Know what you want and don't want, and don't allow others to lead you in a direction that contradicts what you value. Consider making a chastity pledge, and share it with a parent or a friend who will support your commitment. And always ask yourself, Do my choices, even the small ones about what to wear and the language I use, help me to honor the holiness of my body?

Lord, strengthen me as I strive to stay holy in mind, body, and spirit.

Defending against Bullies

I will deal with all your oppressors
 at that time.
And I will save the lame
 and gather the outcast,
and I will change their shame into praise
 and renown in all the earth.

(Zephaniah 3:19)

The Prophet Zephaniah comforted the Israelites when they were being oppressed. He assured them that God would protect the outcast and those who are shunned and help them to rise from shame to glory. Like the Israelites, we too want someone to defend us when we are being mistreated, and we want to be pulled out of misery when we are rejected. Whether the behavior of a bully is aimed at us or at another person, we should take action, reporting the bullying to the appropriate adults. We should also be sure to model respect for others. Does your treatment of your classmates and peers show that all people deserve respect and kindness?

God, you saved the Israelites when they were oppressed. Help all who are bullied, and help me to be a model of respect for all people.

No Orphan in Christ

I will not leave you orphaned; I am coming to you.

(John 14:18)

We have all experienced being lost, such as at a big store or at an amusement park, when we were small. Even if the experience was brief, we can still remember the panic and fear that came with feeling lost, not knowing where our parent was or whether he or she would find us. Being "lost" from our faith can leave us feeling just as alone and disoriented. Without a close connection to God, we can wander without a direction, unsure of where we are or where we should go. By keeping close to God and always staying close to his loving watch, we will always be secure and confident, even when faced with obstacles and worries. If we are feeling "lost" from our faith or from God, we need to ask, What changes can I make to draw me closer to God?

Keep me near you, Jesus, and stay at my side even when I am distracted and wander away from you.

Taking a Stand

> Let us test and examine our ways,
>   and return to the Lord.
> Let us lift up our hearts as well as our hands
>   to God in heaven.
>
> (Lamentations 3:40–41)

It can be easy for us to adopt a group mentality at times. If we are part of a group—whether informal or organized— whose values and behavior result in harm to others, we should either work to help the group change or leave the group. If members of the group are physically placing others in danger, such as by driving under the influence of alcohol or drugs or through aggressive sexual behavior, we have one more obligation: getting an adult involved. The consequences of ignoring violent behavior are grave. When we are in a group, we can ask ourselves, Has what was supposed to be harmless fun turned into violent or risky behavior? If so, we will know it is time to make a change.

As much as I want a group to belong to, Lord, I want to do what is good and holy. I ask your help in being sure all my actions show care for others.

An Attitude for Success

> And every work that he undertook in the service
> of the house of God, and in accordance with the
> law and the commandments, to seek his God, he
> did with all his heart; and he prospered.
>
> (2 Chronicles 31:21)

If we do our schoolwork, chores, extracurricular activities, and our job with an attitude that reflects disdain for these things , we will easily lose the opportunity to grow from these experiences and to honor God through them. However, if we do these same things with a spirit of appreciation for the opportunities God has given us and with a positive attitude, we will proclaim our faith and values and love of God and others. We will find God's hand in all we do, and we will prosper emotionally and spiritually. It may be helpful to ask a friend or parent, "What attitude am I displaying as I do my work?"and make changes where needed.

*My God, inspire in me an attitude of faith and a
desire to glorify you in all I do.*

Holiness and Joy

> Do not deprive yourself of a day's enjoyment;
>> do not let your share of desired good pass by
>> you.

(Sirach 14:14)

When we have a significant person in our lives—a boyfriend or girlfriend—we know that there are right and wrong ways to act. We know what God asks of us and that we are called to chastity and purity. We also know that God wants us to be happy and joyful people. If we are living according to God's commandments, we can certainly experience joy and enjoyment with the person who makes us happy. If we can say, "This relationship is good and holy and I am behaving as I should," then we can enjoy a day of good fun.

God, thank you for the friends you give us and for the enjoyment we can share.

Glorious Deeds

> We will not hide them from their children;
> we will tell to the coming generation
> the glorious deeds of the Lord, and his might,
> and the wonders that he has done.

> (Psalm 78:4)

Sometimes the adults in our lives do not talk openly with young people. Rather than share with us their faith experiences, their questions, and their love of God, they may assume that we are not interested or are not ready to hear. We can encourage adults we trust and care about to share their faith with us by asking questions and sharing our own faith experiences. We can also share our beliefs and questions about our faith with our friends. By creating an atmosphere where hearing about God and talking about our faith is welcome, we can tell and hear about the glorious deeds of the Lord, and we can grow in faith together. Do you encourage others to speak to you about God?

Your deeds are glorious indeed, O God. Open my ears to hear them.

Greed

> Take care! Be on your guard against all kinds of greed.
>
> (Luke 12:15)

We live in a society that places a high value on owning things—lots of things. We feel pressure to own the latest fashions, tech gadgets, sporting gear, and accessories for every occasion. Online, on TV, at the movies, on billboards . . . everywhere we turn we are being told that material possessions are good and will make us so very happy. But if we stop and think about this—the idea that material things equal happiness—we can quickly recognize that this is a trick that marketers use to get us to spend money, often on things we don't need. Greed of any kind is a trap that is easy to fall in to. The next time you see something in a store or in an advertisement that you feel you "have to have," ask yourself, Is this something I truly need? and act accordingly.

God, teach me to be satisfied with the blessings you have given me and to reject greed for material possessions.

Honoring Teachers

> Let the elders who rule well be considered worthy
> of double honor, especially those who labor in
> preaching and teaching.
>
> (1 Timothy 5:17)

Through the care and dedication of our teachers, our minds are nourished. Through their hard work, we gain the knowledge and skills we will need to become independent adults who can contribute to society. Many teachers also help to form our character and nurture in us values that reflect a love of God and others. A teacher who prepares the lessons well, who models a love for God, and who does his or her best to educate students deserves honor. If we ask ourselves, Does my behavior and what I say honor my teachers and show them the respect they deserve? we will live Paul's teaching that those who preach and teach deserve double honor.

You are the greatest teacher, Lord. May I honor all who have been called to teach me and help me grow.

Letting Go of Anger

> He will not always accuse,
>   nor will he keep his anger forever.
> He does not deal with us according to our sins.
>
> (Psalm 103:9–10)

When we are wronged by someone, it is natural to get angry. Sometimes we'll receive an apology and will quickly be able to move forward. At other times, an apology never comes, or even after an apology we still can't let go of our anger. God asks us to be forgiving even when those who wrong us don't seek forgiveness. If we find ourselves asking, Why am I still so mad? or if we cannot let go of anger toward someone and forgive, we can remember how good our God is when we do wrong, and try to respond to others in the same way.

Thank you, forgiving God, for loving me even when I do wrong. Teach me to be forgiving too.

Wise Commitments

> With you is wisdom, she who knows your works
> and was present when you made the world;
> she understands what is pleasing in your sight
> and what is right according to your
> commandments.

(Wisdom of Solomon 9:9)

When we make commitments, we must make judicious choices and act wisely. If we make too many commitments at once, we will likely have a hard time following through on everything. If we commit to something that is out of our scope of knowledge, we may find ourselves in over our heads and unable to do the task justice. And if we commit to something that conflicts with our values or God's commandments, we risk doing harm to ourselves and others. Asking for God's help in choosing what service work or commitments to take on can help us to commit wisely and make a worthwhile contribution. Before making commitments, pray for God's guidance and ask yourself, Will I be serving God and others well by doing this work?

Lord, help me to choose wisely how to serve you and others with my time and talent.

Strength and Courage

> Be strong and courageous; do not be frightened
> or dismayed, for the Lord your God is with you
> wherever you go.
>
> (Joshua 1:9)

As we grow older and grow in knowledge, we can also grow in strength and courage, because our learning can give us confidence and help us conquer our fears. In the same way, the more we know about our faith and about God, the greater our strength to stand firm in our faith and remain true to God's will and his ways even in the face of opposition. As we learn more about God's love for us and what he wants for us and from us, we can become more filled with a quiet courage to always be his faithful people, knowing he is always with us. When we face challenging situations, we can ask ourselves, How can I stay close to God in these difficult circumstances?

God, give me the strength and comfort I need to stay close to you always.

Taking Up the Cross

> He called the crowd with his disciples, and said to them, "If any want to become my followers, let them deny themselves and take up their cross and follow me."
>
> (Mark 8:34)

As we make choices in our daily lives, there are times when a particular choice means denying ourselves and following Christ. For example, if we choose to obey God's will over the pleasure of a sinful behavior, we've denied ourselves and have taken up our cross to follow Christ. Each time we deny ourselves, we grow in virtue, and it becomes easier for us to do the right thing in the future. As we make choices each day, we can check the "rightness" of our decisions by asking, Will this choice bring me closer to Christ?

Lord, give me the strength to take up my cross and follow you in every choice that I make.

Healing through Forgiveness

> And forgive us our debts, as we also have
> forgiven our debtors.
>
> (Matthew 6:12)

When we have done wrong and need forgiveness, nothing is better than receiving forgiveness. We ask for forgiveness over and over, and God will always forgive us. Some friends forgive us over and over, and our parents may do so as well. Just as we seek forgiveness and find healing in receiving it, we should be willing to grant forgiveness to those who hurt or offend us. If we don't forgive, we find ourselves holding on to hurts and fears and other emotions that keep us from having right relationships and healthy thoughts. Forgiveness brings healing to those who receive it and those who grant it. If we find ourselves unwilling to forgive, we can remedy this by asking, How can I bring healing to everyone in this situation?

Merciful God, teach me to seek forgiveness and to be a forgiving person.

Let Your Light Shine

> He said to them, "Is a lamp brought in to be put under the bushel basket, or under the bed, and not on the lampstand?"

> (Mark 4:21)

Imagine if Michelangelo threw away every piece of art he created or if Mother Teresa only thought about helping others but never did it. When we hide our gifts and talents and don't act on our ideas for serving others, we are putting our light under a basket. When we share our gifts and talents, we serve others. Service to others comes in many forms. For example, singing in our school or parish choir serves our faith community, volunteering at a soup kitchen serves those who are poor and in need, and writing letters to politicians and decision makers can serve those who are marginalized. As we begin to decide how and whom to serve, a good start is asking ourselves, What are my talents, and how can I use them to serve others?

Help my light shine in service to others and for your glory, Lord.

Finding the Joy

I think of you on my bed,
    and meditate on you in the watches of the
        night;
for you have been my help,
    and in the shadow of your wings I sing for
        joy.

(Psalm 63:5–7)

Imagine going to bed happy every night; no worries about school or friends. We often lay our head down at night and worry about these things and more. If we ask ourselves each night, Where and when did God help me today? we can focus on those blessings as we go to sleep. We can also look over the day and see all the good in it; the people who have been good to us, the wonders of nature, the love of our family, the company of our friends. If we focus on these good things and thank God for them as we lay down to sleep, our sleep may come easier and our dreams may be songs of joy. Happiness comes when we are grateful for our blessings.

Good and generous Lord, let me meditate on the blessings I receive each day and to end each day with joy.

A Stronghold in the Lord

> The Lord is a stronghold for the oppressed,
>   a stronghold in times of trouble.

> (Psalm 9:9)

When we first learn to swim, we usually hang on to the person teaching us because we know that person will keep us safe. Once we learn to swim, we move through the water freely on our own. Like our childhood swim instructor, God offers us safety and security when we are in situations that frighten us or leave us feeling vulnerable. In times of trouble, we can turn to the Lord as a stronghold, always holding on to us. As we begin to feel any fear or worry, we can ask ourselves, Do I always know that God is at my side, holding on to me and keeping me safe?

You are my stronghold, Lord, and I thank you for being at my side always.

Loving Support

> And he said to him, "Lord, you know everything;
> you know that I love you." Jesus said to him, "Feed
> my sheep."
>
> (John 21:17)

Loving others means that we will help and support them in what is most important in their lives. As Jesus asked Peter about his commitment, Peter felt a little hurt, thinking that Jesus questioned his loyalty and love. When Jesus accepted Peter's answer, he asked him to help carry on his work by leading his people. In our friendships and important relationships, having a serious commitment to helping one another is important. As we think about what loving another means, we can ask, Am I willing to selflessly help this person with what is most important to him or her?

Help me to show true commitment in all my friendships
and to be a source of support, especially in works
that lead to you, Lord.

We Are Not Alone

> For in everything, O Lord, you have exalted and
>   glorified your people,
> and you have not neglected to help them at all
>   times and in all places.
>
> (Wisdom of Solomon 19:22)

Neglect leads to decay. When we neglect a garden, the plants wither. When we neglect our schoolwork, our grades suffer and our goals for the future can fall out of reach. When a child is neglected, he grows weak and afraid of the world around him. Although humans sometimes fail to honor their obligations, God never falls short. He does not neglect his people. Even when we are suffering and feel like we are alone, God is present in our lives. It isn't God who neglects us; instead, we may neglect God or others, resulting in our own or other's suffering. By asking ourselves, Am I neglecting my obligations to myself or to others? we can remember God's presence and our responsibility.

Help me, God, to always be aware of your presence and to do what I can to help others.

Rethinking Popularity

The utterance of a sensible person is sought in the
   assembly,
   and they ponder his words in their minds.

(Sirach 21:17)

When we think of popularity, the first people who come
to mind are typically not the quiet, sensible students who
work hard and get good grades. However, these students
are popular in a different way. They are models of
diligence and responsibility that others can learn from and
aspire to be like in some ways. Being known as someone
who has intelligent, meaningful things to say is a form
of popularity that is worthy of our attention and respect.
As we consider who is popular and wise, asking, Who
speaks as a wise and sensible person? is a good way to
know who is worthy of aspiring to emulate and learn from.

*Lord, help me to be wise and sensible in my speech
and to look up to and emulate those who model these
gifts.*

Light of the World

"I am the light of the world."

(John 8:12)

Being able to turn on a light switch with ease, knowing that there will be light, makes it harder to appreciate the image of Jesus as Light. But imagine a power outage in which you have no ability to bring light into the darkness of night. When we are engulfed in spiritual or emotional darkness that we feel we can't overcome, we can remember that Jesus is the Light who can pierce even the greatest darkness. He is the Light that shows us the way, helps us to see, and calms our fears. When you are worried or afraid and feel surrounded by a heavy darkness, ask yourself, How can I trust and welcome Jesus to be the Light for my life?

Jesus, my Light, light the way for me always, even in times of the deepest darkness.

Matthias Is Called

> And they cast lots for them, and the lot fell on Matthias; and he was added to the eleven apostles.
>
> (Acts of the Apostles 1:26)

We are all called by God to serve him and his people, yet our calling comes in different forms, and can even change in our lifetime. When we are young, we are called to serve God by caring for our siblings and respecting our parents. As we get older, we may be called to serve by participating in a parish ministry or volunteering to help those in need. In adulthood, our call to serve takes the form of a vocation, such as to married life, religious life, or the priesthood. In discovering how we are called to serve, we will likely not be chosen in the way Matthias was chosen. Instead, we have to discern the call through prayer and conversation with God. We can ask God, How can I serve you, Lord? We must also be attentive to God's response and his direction to us.

Lord, help me to discern how you are calling me to serve you.

Service to Workers

> Is not this the carpenter?
>
> (Mark 6:3)

As young people, we have the opportunity to do humble work, such as in a fast-food restaurant. This gives us a chance to learn work ethics and the value of hard work and of the worker. Wherever our future path takes us, and however much success we attain, we should always strive to be mindful of those who labor to provide the goods and services we need, such as service workers and factory workers. We should make it our goal to ensure that these laborers earn fair wages and treatment. We can be informed consumers and ask ourselves, Am I buying products and services from businesses that that treat their workers fairly?

Jesus, help me to treat every worker near and far as I would treat you, the humble carpenter.

Caring for Creation

> Do you have cattle? Look after them.
>
> (Sirach 7:22)

God entrusted creation to us, and directed us to protect it. This means caring for living creatures and their habitats; it means not wasting resources, and not using more of the earth's goods than we need. Taking care of God's creation is our responsibility not just for ourselves, but for the generations that follow us. As you ponder your responsibility to care for the earth and its resources, ask yourself, What are some ways I can show respect for all the wonders of creation God has given to me?

Creator God, thank you for all the goodness of the earth that you have given to me. Teach me to care for your creation selflessly.

A Fashionable Spirit

> Rather, let your adornment be the inner self with the lasting beauty of a gentle and quiet spirit, which is very precious in God's sight.
>
> (1 Peter 3:4)

Wearing the latest fashions is important to some of us. If we do so in a spirit of humility and because we like the fashions, it is okay. If we go along with a fad or style because we are trying to fit in or because we are uncomfortable with who we really are, then we should rethink our intentions. Our first focus should be on ensuring our inner beauty—making sure our spirit is healthy and in harmony with God and with others. When we attain this harmony, our confidence and inner peace will be evident, and external beauty will follow.

God, help me to attain the inner beauty and the outward confidence that come from being in harmony with you.

A Reflection of God

> The Lord will guide you continually,
>   and satisfy your needs in parched places,
>   and make your bones strong;
> and you shall be like a watered garden,
>   like a spring of water,
>   whose waters never fail.

(Isaiah 58:11)

When we look in the mirror, we sometimes see a reflection that we are critical of, that we want to change. We may wish for different hair or a different smile. Because our self-esteem is linked to what we see in the mirror, this makes it hard to feel good about ourselves and to see what God sees in us. Having confidence in our appearance is important. This confidence can start by knowing that God loves us and cares for us and wants us to know love and happiness, and that he wants us to love and care for ourselves and to live as his children. Asking ourselves, What can I do to be the best me? means taking care of our physical appearance as well as ensuring that we are a reflection of God's love in all we do.

I pray that my life reflects your love in all ways, Lord.

By Name

> Peace to you. The friends send you their greetings.
> Greet the friends there, each by name.
>
> (3 John 1:15)

When we are in a noisy crowd, we don't hear every word being said, but when our name is called, our ears perk up. Our name is a great signifier of who we are, and being called by name is one way we feel accepted. Of course we call our family members and our friends by name. But what about others in our class, in our neighborhood, and in groups and teams we belong to? Do we take time to know the names of those we might perceive as different from ourselves, those who don't fit in with our circle of friends and family? Take time to know those whom you might not normally gravitate to socially, and learn names when you can. And ask yourself, Can I bridge the distance that separates me from another person simply by calling him or her by name?

God, may I remember that by calling others by name
I honor and accept them just as you accept me.

Bear Friends' Burdens

> Bear one another's burdens, and in this way you will fulfill the law of Christ.
>
> (Galatians 6:2)

When we think of friendship, we don't usually also think of the word *burden*. Friendships are a source of comfort and joy, not hardship. Yet true friendship also sometimes means bearing burdens. Friends share one another's burdens—whether the burden is temporary, such as the difficulty of a breakup, or more lasting, such as a physical disability. When we provide comfort and support to our friends when they face a burden, we answer Jesus' call to love one another. Just as we sometimes ask ourselves whom among our friends we can truly count on, we can also ask ourselves, Am I a true friend who is loyal and supportive even at the times when a friendship requires selflessness and patience?

God, who helps me to bear my burdens, help me to be a source of comfort and support to my friends when they are burdened.

Peer Pressure Slaves

> For freedom Christ has set us free. Stand firm, therefore, and do not submit again to a yoke of slavery.
>
> (Galatians 5:1)

Anything that prevents us from being true to our faith and our values is a form of slavery. Peer pressure, then, is a form of slavery, because if we succumb to it, we allow it to control our choices instead of basing them on what we truly believe and value. As we hear in the Letter to the Galatians, we are free when we are with Christ. If we draw on that freedom when faced with peer pressure, we can choose to turn away from the slavery of peer pressure. The next time we are faced with negative choices by our peers, we can ask ourselves, Is this decision moving me in the direction of Christ's freedom or toward the slavery of peer pressure?

Christ, who provides freedom to all, help me to make the decisions that lead me toward the freedom that comes from you and not into the slavery of peer pressure.

Family Values

> Be subject to one another out of reverence for Christ.
>
> (Ephesians 5:21)

We are all familiar with the term *family values*. At its most basic level, the term can be restated as "value your family." In Ephesians we are given instructions that may challenge the norms of our time, but at their core these instructions simply exhort family members to love one another, support one another, respect one another, and lead one another to Christ through the way we live. The next time we grow impatient or angry with a brother, a sister, or a parent, we can recall the words of Ephesians and ask ourselves, Is what I am saying or doing or how I feel a reflection of my reverence for Christ and respect for my family members?

As I desire to show reverence for you, Christ, help me also to show reverence for my family.

Jesus' Compassion

> And Jesus said, "Neither do I condemn you. Go your way, and from now on do not sin again."
>
> (John 8:11)

No matter what the sin, Jesus' response to genuine repentance was never condemnation but always forgiveness. The woman in this story was treated in exactly the opposite way by the townspeople and religious leaders. They shamed and humiliated her by bringing her before everyone, and then threatened to stone her to death. (However, they could not carry out this threat. Under the Roman occupation, only the Roman government could pronounce a death sentence.) In our culture too, we seem to enjoy the humiliation of others. Is this something Jesus would approve? The next time headlines proclaim the sins of another, or news stories dwell on wrongdoing, ask yourself: Do I join in condemnation? Or do I say a prayer, bringing this person to Jesus not in condemnation but in compassion?

Jesus, keep me from rejoicing in others' wrongdoings. Lead me to rejoice in your forgiving love.

Let Gossip Die

> Have you heard something? Let it die with you.
> Be brave, it will not make you burst!
>
> (Sirach 19:10)

When we hear some juicy gossip, we have choices regarding what to do with the information. We know that the right thing to do is to not spread the gossip, but we may be tempted to share it so we can enjoy the reactions of those we tell, or to hurt the reputation of someone we don't like. Worse, we might be tempted to share the gossip via a social networking site, where hundreds or thousands of people might learn about it. Although the temptation might be strong, when we have some juicy gossip about someone else, we should ask ourselves: What would Jesus tell me? Would he want me to spread the gossip, or would he gently instruct me to let it die?

God of wisdom love, help me learn to always act with others in a spirit of charity, and to resist the temptation to spread hurtful gossip.

Find Safety and Celebrate It

> Then the prophet Miriam, Aaron's sister, took a tambourine in her hand; and all the women went out after her with tambourines and with dancing.
>
> (Exodus 15:20)

God's way of providing safety to us isn't usually as spectacular as the parting of the Red Sea, the event Miriam was celebrating. Yet every day God provides a safe place for us in the form of our faith community, in our homes with our families, and amid the comfort and security of our friends. If at times we find ourselves in a dangerous situation, or threatened by the behavior of others, we can turn to those who love us and care for us, in our faith community, at school, or among our family or friends, for help and support. If we are ever in need of this safe place, we just need to ask ourselves, Whom is God sending to help me and protect me? Once we have found safety, we can rejoice in God's protection and goodness.

Thank you, God, for keeping me safe.

Be Light

> For all who do evil hate the light and do not
> come to the light, so that their deeds may not be
> exposed.

> (John 3:20)

In the Book of Genesis, the first thing Adam and Eve did
after their sin was hide. This seems to be a natural human
reaction—to hide ourselves and keep our wrongdoing
from others. Sometimes we help others to hide, and this
can result in grave injustice, especially if a significant hurt
is involved. Keeping things in the dark will help no one.
As hard as it is, speaking out when we or others are hurt
is necessary to bring justice and healing to all parties.
The person who was hurt needs to heal and may need
spiritual, medical, or psychological assistance. The person
who did the hurting also needs to heal, both spiritually
and psychologically, through a process of reconciliation
and restitution. As you encounter those who are in either
situation, bring it to the light.

*Lord of light, may I live in your light and be willing to
speak out for those who are hurting.*

The Path of Faith

> Teach me to do your will,
>   for you are my God.
> Let your good spirit lead me
>   on a level path.
>
>   (Psalm 143:10)

When walking on a rocky path, we can easily trip or turn an ankle. A level path on a trail means that someone came before us and cleared some of the rocks and roots away. In our faith we have those trailblazers too. Yet we do not find them standing alongside the trail keeping us from veering off; it is our responsibility to stay on the trail. Likewise, in our faith tradition we have those who go before us to open the path of Christian life for us. We have our own gift of free will. We can choose to stay on the path or to veer off in another direction. As we walk on our faith path, we can ask ourselves, Am I on the path that leads to true life, or am I veering off to where I may trip or fall?

Lord, show me your path and help me to stay on it. Thank you for those who have opened the path ahead of me.

Waiting for Love

And now, O Lord, what do I wait for?
My hope is in you.

(Psalm 39:7)

In the past it was considered normal for young people to marry after high school. Young men were expected to have a steady job and young women were expected to "make the home." This is not the case today. These days, college or post-high-school training is often necessary. So it may not be wise to focus on one person too quickly, when "settling down" is not an option. Should we then put relationships on hold? The answer is: Put hope in God. Putting our trust in God about dating may seem farfetched. However, if we trust God in other aspects of life, why not trust God in our relationships? If we find ourselves worrying about a future partner, the questions to ask are, How can I put this concern in God's hands? and What constructive things can I do instead of obsessing about the future?

God, help me to trust you in all aspects of my life, especially with my concern for a future marriage partner.

Faith and Peace

If it is possible, so far as it depends on you, live peaceably with all.

(Romans 12:18)

Even if we were very little, or not even born, we know that September 11 is a day of mourning. It is a day of remembrance and prayer for those who lost their lives in the terrorist attacks that took place in 2001. On this day, we pause to remember those who were injured or died and their families. Finding hope in such an event is like trying to find one hidden pine needle in a forest. To move forward, the survivors, the families of those who died, and the whole world has drawn on faith. Our faith reminds us that even those who have died still live, and calls us to live peacefully with all. As we remember this day, we are called to put aside hatred and revenge, and to ask ourselves, How can I bring peace to others?

God of peace, help me to be a person of compassion and love today and every day.

Rich or Poor?

> Better to be poor and walk in integrity
>> than to be crooked in one's ways even though
>> rich.

(Proverbs 28:6)

Games of "This or That" are fun when we get to consider being very pretty or very popular. It is also easy to answer when there are two opposite factors. When asked, "Choose between rich and poor," the usual answer is "Rich!" Or when asked, "Choose between integrity and crookedness," most answer "Integrity." However, if we were asked with both factors together, "Poor with integrity?" or "Crooked and rich?" we may stop and have to think twice about our answer. However, in Proverbs we are given the only correct answer. Being crooked means we'd be dishonest and unfair, and would bring untold harm to others. (Just think what would have happened to the town in *It's a Wonderful Life* if the crooked bankers had been in charge!) Those who walk in integrity walk with Christ.

God of integrity, may money and possessions never tempt me to compromise my integrity.

School or Prison

> To a senseless person education is fetters on his
> feet,
> and like manacles on his right hand.
>
> (Sirach 21:19)

"I wish I never had to go back to school!" Words like these indicate that the educational process is not always an easy one. Feeling that education is an imprisonment may be the result of many factors. Learning disabilities can frustrate some students. If that is the case, solutions can be found through special modalities or adaptations. If we are in that situation, we need to get the help we need by going to a counselor or learning specialist. But if we are feeling that school is a "prison" because we just don't like it, we can ask why. Are we falling behind in class? Are difficulties at home interfering with our concentration? We can consider our attitude toward school and can ask ourselves: If my attitude is negative, why is it? Can I speak with someone to get help in making school more meaningful to me?

God of all knowledge, help me to open my mind and heart to learning.

God Listens

> Then my tongue shall tell of your righteousness
> and of your praise all day long.
>
> (Psalm 35:28)

It feels good to vent. If we have a trusted friend, we tell them what is bothering us. We talk it over together and then we are able to move on. When that happens, we sincerely thank that friend. God is such a friend. As the writer of Psalm 35 vents about his enemies and hardships, he ends with praise for God. In the same way, God helps and comforts us, and we too sing of his wonderful deeds. If we find ourselves in need of venting, God is only a prayer away. By asking ourselves, How has God helped me through hardships and in difficulties? we can start a good conversation.

God, whose name I praise, thank you for hearing me in my difficult times. Thank you for helping me to move on.

Renewing Commitments

At that moment the cock crowed for the second time. Then Peter remembered that Jesus had said to him, "Before the cock crows twice, you will deny me three times." And he broke down and wept.

(Mark 14:72)

When Peter heard that rooster crowing, he realized that he had broken the commitment he made to Jesus. Denial and betrayal do almost irreparable damage to any relationship—damage that is not easy to heal. However, we know that Jesus forgave Peter and entrusted him to be the leader of his followers. We may feel terrible if we damage a friendship or break a commitment, or if someone does so to us. At those times we need to remember that we are all human, and there are times when we fail to reach others' expectations, or even our own. We need to remember the power of forgiveness and the possibility of a fresh start. The former is always possible; the latter requires a free and mutual decision on both sides.

Jesus, you were horribly betrayed. May I learn how to forgive from you.

Do Not Be Afraid

> Then Jesus said to them, "Do not be afraid; go
> and tell my brothers to go to Galilee; there they
> will see me."
>
> (Matthew 28:10)

When we are faced with a scary situation, we can find
it hard to think clearly. We might even experience "brain
freeze." In learning what to do in an emergency, we are
taught to use repetition and role-play. As we practice,
over and over again, how to administer CPR, we train our
brains to take over in an actual emergency. If that occurs,
repetition kicks in, just as in practice. In "emergencies of
the spirit," like times of fear, temptation, or anxiety, it is
helpful to have short Scripture phrases or prayers to turn
to. The phrase "Do not be afraid" is one that will come in
handy when we hear ourselves asking, What can I say to
calm myself down? Through repetition, we will know it by
heart. When we need it, it will be ready to help us.

Jesus, you are with me always. I will not be afraid.

Faith Foundation

> That one is like a man building a house, who dug deeply and laid the foundation on rock; when a flood arose, the river burst against that house but could not shake it, because it had been well built.
>
> (Luke 6:48)

A beautiful building can have all the bells and whistles, but a good contractor or engineer is most concerned about what is underneath. How strong is the foundation and the inner supports? Like a good contractor, Jesus is concerned about what is underneath us, what supports us. Are we standing on him, the Rock, and on the Mass and the Sacraments, religious education, good friends, and prayer? Or are we content to throw together a life built on sandy soil, a life that the least bit of stormy weather will destroy? Laying a foundation of faith will serve us well when life's storms come our way. As we learn and grow and pray, we can ask ourselves, What am I doing now that will help to lay a solid foundation of faith for my life?

Jesus, my Rock, help me to build a solid foundation on you.

Grace of Forgiveness

> For sin will have no dominion over you, since you are not under law but under grace.
>
> (Romans 6:14)

Dominion means power or control. Sin exists, but because of Baptism, we live in grace. Every Sacrament does what it says it will do: renew grace, God's life, in us. In the Sacrament of Reconciliation, we are given the grace of forgiveness from God through the words and actions of the priest. What a gift this is! We are human and the tendency to sin is always with us. Yet knowing that sin hurts God, ourselves, and others, we, with the help of God's grace, try not to sin and to seek forgiveness when we do. In our weakness, one sin can lead to another, and eventually we may begin to feel powerless. If we are feeling that sin is beginning to have dominion over us, we can ask, Is it time to experience the grace and peace of the Sacrament of Penance and Reconciliation?

Thank you, Christ my Savior, for the grace of Baptism, and for the possibility of God's forgiveness in the Sacrament of Penance and Reconciliation.

The Capable Person

> She opens her hand to the poor,
> and reaches out her hands to the needy.
>
> (Proverbs 31:20)

Demonstrating capability is knowing what to do in certain situations, showing skill in particular areas, and living up to our potential. What does it mean in areas of faith? A capable Christian is a lifelong learner in areas of faith, Scripture, and spirituality. A capable Christian looks for opportunities to be part of a solution rather than part of a problem. A capable Christian opens hands to the poor by helping those who are less fortunate and also by advocating for them in other ways. A capable Christian reaches out to the needy by donating clothing or writing politicians to change laws. When deciding on actions to take, we can ask ourselves, What would a capable Christian do in this situation?

Thank you, God, for giving me the skills of a capable Christian. Help me to use them in service to others.

Happiness Shared

> Let none of us fail to share in our revelry;
> everywhere let us leave signs of enjoyment,
> because this is our portion, and this our lot.
>
> (Wisdom of Solomon 2:9)

Celebrating with friends is a natural way to express our joy. When a friend is accepted into college, wins a game, or has another great experience, it is natural to want to share the joy. Shared joy brings happiness. As people of faith, we celebrate God's love together; coming together each week to celebrate Mass is one way to share the happiness our faith gives. As we experience sad or lonely times, remembering the times of shared enjoyment can start us back on the road toward happiness. As we seek those starting points, we can ask ourselves, When was the last time I shared in another's joy and successes? and remember that experience as a way to finding our own path to happiness.

God of joy, thank you for the happiness I find in my faith, friends, and family.

Lemons or Lemonade?

Let your steadfast love, O Lord, be upon us,
even as we hope in you.

(Psalm 33:22)

Some people are naturally optimistic; they are the ones who, when life gives them lemons, make lemonade. Being optimistic comes harder for some of us though. Sometimes it is hard to see the possibilities in difficult situations we encounter. If we find ourselves getting stuck in negative thoughts and worries, the Psalms are a rich source of hope. Many Psalms remind us to have hope, to trust the Lord, and to keep a positive perspective. The verse above reminds us to rely on God's steadfast love and to hope in him. This would be a good verse to commit to memory. As we find ourselves needing a little hope and encouragement, we can ask, "Have I looked to the Psalms as a source of hope?"

God, my hope, when life gives me lemons, help me to make lemonade!

Circle of Love

> Happy are those who saw you
>   and were adorned with your love! For we
>   also shall surely live.
>
> (Sirach 48:11)

Being loved has its rewards. Those who love us put up with the crazy and sometimes hurtful things we do. We return and share this love in a variety of ways, thus expanding our circle of love. Genuine love makes us part of something bigger than ourselves: the love of God. This verse addresses the prophet Elijah, who was a significant figure in the history of the Jewish people, and, as a model for John the Baptist, is important for Christians as well. Those who were in Elijah's circle of love were part of something very big: God's plan for our salvation. God's plan of love resulted in Jesus Christ's birth, death, and Resurrection, giving us life forever. So if we are feeling unloved, we just need to ask ourselves: "How is God's love expressed through those around me, and how am I expressing it to others?"

God of love, help me to share in your life by sharing your love with others.

Suffering for Faith

> Therefore I endure everything for the sake of the elect, so that they may also obtain the salvation that is in Christ Jesus, with eternal glory.
>
> (2 Timothy 2:10)

Even in modern times, people suffer for religious freedom and for basic rights. God doesn't want us to have to suffer, but suffering is sometimes a consequence of a faith-filled life. We may not be thrown in jail for professing our faith, but we may have to put up with a peer making fun of us for going to church or being part of a youth group. We may not be threatened with death for believing in God, but we may sometimes be inconvenienced by meeting our obligation to participate in the Sunday Eucharist. And then there may sometimes be a few disparaging remarks about Catholicism to suffer through! If we do have to suffer, even in a small way, we can ask ourselves, How does this experience help me to grow stronger as a person of faith?

Lord Jesus, if I have to suffer for my faith, help me to grow stronger because of it.

Compassion and Patience

> But when the crowds heard it, they followed him
> on foot from the towns.

> (Matthew 14:13)

In today's world, popular stars are followed around by paparazzi and fans. This can be annoying and sometimes even threatening. Even ordinary young people can get overwhelmed by attention. Jesus' popularity resulted in a crowd of followers who wanted to be around him as much as possible—even when he was trying to have some quiet time. Jesus' response was to preach, heal, and ensure that his followers had enough to eat. Popularity should never be a goal for its own sake. If we happen to be popular with others, we should draw on Jesus' example of compassion and patience. Of course if someone's constant attention frightens us or makes us uncomfortable, we need to ask for help. But, as caring Christians, we need to understand and accept the challenges and joys of life, whether that includes being popular or not.

Thank you, Jesus, for your compassion and patience. Help me to follow you!

Vine and Branches

"I am the vine, you are the branches."

(John 15:5)

In describing himself and his mission, Jesus often used these everyday objects and images. Describing himself as a vine was a great way for his followers to "get" who he, Jesus, was. In Jesus' time, people grew their own food. People knew what a vine was and how the branches were attached to it. They would have easily understood the image Jesus presented. In fact, the vines and the branches of a grape vine are so intertwined, sharing the same life, that they look very much alike. Was this what Jesus was trying to say in using this image? And, a vine bears fruit for others. We, as the branches of Jesus, the vine, are expected to bear fruit too. We do this by living a faith-filled life, praising God, sharing in his love, and serving others. What fruit are we bearing? We can check by asking ourselves, How do I share the life and love of Jesus with others?

Jesus, True Vine, help me to be a branch that bears good fruit.

Timothy

> Do not neglect the gift that is in you, which was given to you through prophecy with the laying on of hands by the council of elders.
>
> (1 Timothy 4:14)

When we are happy with a material gift, we use it and share it. We are also given nonmaterial gifts and talents. These need to be used and shared also. Imagine receiving a call from a talent scout telling us that we have a singing contract, or from a college recruiter that we have won a full scholarship. We probably wouldn't forget to respond and accept! Yet some of us are given a special call from God and neglect to respond. Timothy was a young leader, chosen by Paul himself. At times Timothy may have felt like giving the gift of leadership back to Paul! But Paul encouraged him to use his gifts of service. When we hear the call to service, we need to ask ourselves, Is this the call I am reminded to nurture, not neglect?

Lord Jesus, thank you for Timothy's young leadership. Help me to hear and respond to your call in my life.

Hold Fast to Justice

> But as for you, return to your God,
>   hold fast to love and justice,
>   and wait continually for your God.
>
> (Hosea 12:6)

We hold tight to a friend's hand when we are in a big crowd, careful not to get separated from each other. Holding fast and tight to values and principles is important as well. Just as we make every effort to hold on to that friend's hand, we can make every effort to hold on to the things that our God and our faith tradition consider important. By holding on to them, we are more likely to carry out actions that reflect them. When we give attention to those with few friends, help those struggling with poverty, or work to end hunger and disease, we hold fast to love and justice. How can you hold fast to love and justice in practical ways?

Lord God, help me to hold fast to love and justice in my thoughts, words, and actions.

Protect Creation

> Then the Lord looked upon the earth,
> and filled it with his good things.
>
> (Sirach 16:29)

As we interact with nature, we experience all the good things God created. For those of us at the coasts or near the Great Lakes, we experience the beauty and power of these great waters, created by God. Others of us experience the majesty of the mountains; others know the intricate beauty of the prairies and deserts. Even if we live in cities, we have trees, parks, sparkling fountains, and even zoos in which to see and enjoy the Creator's good things. Just as we take pride in our creation or ownership, and are careful to care for the good things we make or own, God certainly doesn't want his good creation destroyed or damaged. What have you done, and what can you do to protect God's good things?

Thank you, God and Creator, for all of your good things. Help me to protect them.

Child of God

> See what love the Father has given us, that we
> should be called children of God; and that is what
> we are.
>
> (1 John 3:1)

As we list all of our personal characteristics, we usually start with the easy ones: I am a student, I am of mixed ancestry, etc. We might include some sort of regional association: I am an American or a Los Angelino. We may even include our strengths: I play football or tennis. And most of us will list: I am a Catholic. Yet we most likely won't list: I am a child of God. And yet that characteristic is the most important one and should go to the top of the list! What a great identity, given, as John notes in the verse above, with great love. It is often said that the teen years are the years for exploring identity. If we ever wonder who we really are in this multifaceted world, we just need to stop and remind ourselves of this basic truth: I am a child of God.

God, I am so thankful to be your child. May I always reflect your goodness and love in the way I live.

Made by God

> Your hands have made and fashioned me.
>
> (Psalm 119:73)

Cheap T-shirts fall apart. Many of our electronic items aren't worth fixing because it is just cheaper to replace them. We have a lot of disposable items—even an excess of them. We toss trash away on a daily basis. But we keep and take care of the special objects that are handmade, artistic, or sentimental reminders from special people. We too are special—made by God, fashioned as his special and unique creations. As the saying has it, God doesn't make junk. When we call ourselves ugly or stupid, or think thoughts like, I'm not good enough, we are tossing out something God has made as if it were junk. In contrast, as we see our faults and failings, we can repeat the Psalm verse above and ask ourselves, If God made and fashioned me, how can I honor myself as his creation?

God, Creator of me, the handmade one and only me, thank you for the gift of myself. Help me to honor you by honoring myself.

Acceptance

> "Let us go with you, for we have heard that God is
> with you."
>
> (Zechariah 8:23)

When we accept others, it is often because they have interests similar to ours. Sometimes we are the ones hoping to be accepted by a potential friend or group. But how would we feel if the sole reason for rejection was due to our faith in God? This was the situation of the Jewish people. They longed to be like other nations, but their faith in the one true God set them apart. Yet the prophet assured them that the others would not only accept them but seek them out because their faith in God brought hope. Our faith in God gives us a welcoming and accepting spirit. If we are hoping to be accepted by others, we might ask ourselves, Do the people I hope to have as friends seem to have God's welcoming and accepting spirit? If not, maybe it would be best to look elsewhere for support and friendship.

God of all, help me to be a person who accepts others in a welcoming spirit. May I in turn be accepted by others in the same way.

Faith-Filled Friends

> And when they could not bring him to Jesus because of the crowd, they removed the roof above him; and after having dug through it, they let down the mat on which the paralytic lay.
>
> (Mark 2:4)

We say to our friends, "I'd do anything for you!" And if a friend gets really sick, for example, we figure out ways to do what we can to help her or him during the healing process. The friends of the paralyzed man had so much faith that they not only brought him to Jesus, they climbed up on a roof, cut a hole in it, and lowered their friend down to get closer to Jesus. Because of their faith, Jesus responded by healing the paralytic. Imagine what our faith can do for our friends! By praying for them, inviting them to parish activities, and supporting them on their faith journey, we are like the friends of the paralytic. This is an important part of our answer to the question, What would I do for a friend?

Jesus, you blessed the friends of the paralytic by healing him. Bless me when I help and support my friends.

Don't Let Them

Let no one deceive you with empty words.

(Ephesians 5:6)

Others may persuade us to "go along and get along," but we are the ones who choose to follow the crowd. Negative peer pressure can be hard to resist, but, in the end, the decision is always up to us. Allowing others to make decisions for us is a way of giving up. We give up our voice, our dreams, and sometimes even our very self. The writer of the Letter to the Ephesians warns us to think before we act on "empty words." In our own day, the empty words of flattery, attempted coercion, and risky ideas may sound like the road to popularity, self-satisfaction, and enjoyment. But empty words are the same now as they were in biblical times: They lead to our turning from God and from our own self-respect. We can avoid situations if we stop and think, Am I letting others make decisions for me, or am I following my own truth?

Let me listen only to the words that lead to you, Lord Jesus, and to reliance on my own truth.

Family Trees

> An account of the genealogy of Jesus the Messiah, the son of David, the son of Abraham.
>
> (Matthew 1:1)

Genealogy is a popular pastime for many people. They find enjoyment and great interest in discovering their roots. Many of us have relatives who help us to discover our roots, either by telling us stories or by compiling documents showing our family's history. Discovering where we came from helps us to know who we are today. Jesus' family tree was recounted in the Gospel of Matthew. Why? Because Matthew wrote to a Jewish-Christian audience, and he wanted these followers of Jesus to connect with Jesus' family and their own Jewish tradition. Yet Ruth, who was a Gentile, was also included in Matthew's list, as the message of Jesus is open to all. If we think about our own family tree, how would we answer the question, What stories do I know of my family, and whom can I ask to learn more?

Jesus, our Messiah and Savior, thank you for bringing me into your family of faith.

Sex and Sinning

> He does not deal with us according to our sins,
> nor repay us according to our iniquities.
>
> (Psalm 103:10)

We are often harder on ourselves than anyone else. When we fail at something, we replay the event over and over in our memory. If we commit a serious sin, we are separated from God and often feel that pain—in stomachaches and sleepless nights. Even if we are forgiven by God in confession, we find it hard to forgive ourselves. When we find ourselves in this painful situation because of a decision regarding sex, there may be even more complications, physically and emotionally. Remembering that God does not deal with us according to our sins, but loves us and wants the best for us, is reassuring. After setting ourselves straight with God through the Sacrament of Penance and Reconciliation, we can ask ourselves, Who else can I turn to for help in this situation? and then take the next right steps.

God, through all my mistakes, you love me. Thank you for being with me as I deal with the consequences of sin.

Dealing with Enemies

Now my head is lifted up
above my enemies all around me.

(Psalm 27:6)

Bullies are enemies (hopefully, only temporary ones) who seek to gain power over us with fear and threats. The best way to deal with bullies is by telling authorities, parents, and friends what is going on. Having a network of people who can help us to deal with bullies is a good coping mechanism. Sometimes a firm response like "Leave me alone! I don't have to listen to you!" reasserts boundaries. Another way to cope is to find comfort and hope in Scripture. At the same time, we can realize that bullies need help too (their quest for power over others is evidence of a severe lack in their own lives) and would benefit from our prayers, as Jesus recommended (see Matthew 5:44). By asking ourselves, If I am being bullied, or someone else is, how can I help bring it to an end? we can move forward with our head held high.

Thank you, God, for putting people in my life who love and respect me.

Christ's Light

> He has rescued us from the power of darkness
> and transferred us into the kingdom of his beloved
> Son.
>
> (Colossians 1:13)

When we are in total darkness, a certain fear and even a paralysis may set in. Total darkness is disorienting. We don't know in which direction to turn, so we just stop moving. And then the lights come back on! We are free to move and go forward. The fear and paralysis of total darkness is a great analogy to life without God. But we have been given a light for our way—the light of Christ. The love and light of Christ is our kingdom. Because of Christ's light, we can move forward in our lives with peace and joy. Because of Christ's light, we now know to turn in the direction of love. God's love is never absent. When we wonder where God is amid the darkness, we need to turn toward the light of Christ as we ask, Where do I need light in my life?

Light of Christ, be the light that frees me from my fear and shows me the best direction for my life.

Inner Hunger

> You shall eat, but not be satisfied, and there shall
> be a gnawing hunger within you.
>
> (Micah 6:14)

Those who commit violence think they will be satisfied by
their actions. They are usually trying to fill a hunger, or
lack in themselves, that they wrongly think can be filled by
violence or by abusing others. Most teenagers are hungry
for something deep and lasting: love, acceptance, or self-
esteem. Sadly some choose to meet those needs through
violence. And they may recruit others to join them. For
some of us, resisting gangs and the gang lifestyle is an
everyday concern. If this is our concern, we need to seek
help from parents, friends, and the proper authorities.
Finding safe places to go after school is one way to find
support. If we know friends who are tempted to join a
violent gang, we can ask ourselves, How can I help? We
can pray for them and offer them friendship and support.

*Lord Jesus, you understand all our needs. Help us to
meet our needs by following you.*

Faith and Love

> And may the Lord make you increase and abound in love for one another and for all, just as we abound in love for you.
>
> (1 Thessalonians 3:12)

Love is a word with many meanings. It is a word repeated throughout Jesus' teachings and in the letters of the New Testament. What does it mean? Gospel love, faith-filled love, is a gift of self. When we participate in faith activities at our church and schools, we share this love. When we serve the poor and help others through justice and service activities, we witness to this love. When we lead prayers in our youth groups, act as a peer leader, and lead faith-filled lives, we spread this love. As we study, play, and pray, we can ask ourselves, Does this activity help me to grow in faith and in self-giving love?

Lord of love, help me to grow in self-giving love. Help and extend this love to all as a reflection of your love for me and for all your people.

Self-Control and Dating

Likewise, urge the younger men [and women] to be self-controlled.

(Titus 2:6)

Self-control is a gift of the Holy Spirit. It involves both feeling and thinking: first, paying attention to our feelings and then deciding whether to act on them. How many opportunities do we have to practice self-control while dating? We have an opportunity to practice it even before the moment we say yes to a date. For example, if someone asks us to a formal dance, we may not really want to date that person. Practicing self-control, we can be honest with that person and perhaps still be able to go as friends. We know that we have opportunities to practice self-control when we are indeed attracted to someone, and when he or she is attracted to us. We need self-control to put our feelings into perspective before we decide to do something we aren't ready for or know is wrong.

Holy Spirit, help me to approach every decision in life with both heart and mind. Help me to practice your gift of self-control.

God's Loving Protection

> But let all who take refuge in you rejoice;
>   let them ever sing for joy.
> Spread your protection over them,
>   so that those who love your name may exult
>   in you.

(Psalm 5:11)

When a sudden rainstorm strikes, we are grateful to find shelter. If we are having a bad day, finding companionship in a youth room or other safe place brings us joy and hope again. The places of refuge in our lives can be symbols of God's love. But God himself is a refuge who is always with us. Does God's protection mean that nothing bad will ever happen? No. We will experience the consequences of evil and just plain thoughtlessness in our lives. But God will be there to help us through it, for he sent us Jesus, his only Son, as proof of his love. The next time we wonder if God cares, we just need to ask ourselves, How can I remember that God is with me here and now?

Thank you, God, for your loving protection, and for the gift of your Son, Jesus Christ, as proof of your love.

Wisdom or Money

> If riches are a desirable possession in life, what is richer than wisdom, the active cause of all things?
>
> (Wisdom of Solomon 8:5)

Many of us would say that love is more important than money, and some of us would say that health is more important than money, but who of us would say that wisdom is more desirable than money? Wisdom can't buy anything. We can't hug it. It can't do us any good if we are sick, can it? Yet wisdom causes all other good things to happen. It makes sense, then, to desire wisdom first. When we have wisdom and get money, we'll know what to do with it. When we have both wisdom and love, and then get money, we'll want to share it. Wisdom and love are indeed more important than money. We are responsible for prioritizing what we value. If we ask ourselves, What do I place in value above money? we'll begin to see our strength or weakness in this area.

God, grant me the wisdom to seek you and your love above everything else. Help me to share what I have with others who have less.

Diligent or Lazy?

The hand of the diligent will rule,
  while the lazy will be put to forced labor.

(Proverbs 12:24)

We hear it all the time: "Do your work. Don't be lazy. You'll end up without a job." Being diligent about our studies, as well as in other areas of life, will pay off. This seems to be a simple matter of cause and effect. However, diligence or laziness are more than roads taken or not taken. They are character traits, which means they become part of us. They become who we are in some way, and in themselves can shape the future. Both good and bad habits are hard to break! By doing our best to take advantage of the opportunities given to us to learn and grow, we will eventually be able to rule our own lives independently and purposefully, and to make a positive impact on the lives of others as well. As we study we need to ask ourselves, Am I being diligent or lazy?

Lord of all, I pray for diligence in all I do. Help me to move forward on the road to independence and purpose.

Constructive Anger

I am afraid that my work for you may have been wasted.

(Galatians 4:11)

When we study with someone, helping them to understand a concept, and then watch them not caring and not trying in class, we feel like the work we've done is wasted. And we get angry at the person for wasting our time. Paul was feeling a little like this with the Galatians. He had spent a lot of effort in sharing Christ's message and the Christian way of life with them. Then he heard that they were not following through. As we see, he expresses his anger not in violence or in abandonment but in encouraging them to get back on track. If others bring out anger in us because of their behavior, we can help them by asking ourselves, How can I be constructive and help my friends to get back on track?

Jesus, my friend and brother, enable me to help my friends in their need. I want the best for them just as you want the best for me. Help me to turn my anger into constructive encouragement to get back on track.

Commitments

> Stand by your agreement and attend to it,
>   and grow old in your work.
>
>   (Sirach 11:20)

When someone commits a life to God through the
Sacrament of Holy Orders, or to another person through
Matrimony, the commitment is lifelong. Those who make
this commitment know they are signing up for something
they'll be doing until death or well into old age. Other
commitments may not be lifelong but deserve serious
consideration. As we mature, we face more and more
serious decisions about our relationships and sexuality,
our education and career. If we enter into commitments
with the same serious thought of those making a lifelong
commitment, we will probably be better at making
decisions less impulsively. As we make important
decisions, we can reflect on these questions for help: Is
this a decision I will be happy with when I am older? Does
it lead me to the future I am hoping for?

*God of promise and fulfillment, help me to make only
those life-giving commitments I am willing to keep.*

Exile

> Hear, O Lord, our prayer and our supplication,
> and for your own sake deliver us, and grant us
> favor in the sight of those who have carried us into
> exile.
>
> (Baruch 2:14)

Many of us know the pain of exile. We may sometimes feel exiled from society, our peers, or our family. Feeling exiled includes fears of never being included, of not finding the right place to fit in, or of never being understood. Telling a trusted adult or friend how we feel is one way to start returning from exile. In addition, we can, like the people of the Old Testament, call on the Lord for help. The exiled people of Israel were faced with the loss of their homes and the making of new ones in a foreign land. They hoped to fit in to their new situation and yet not leave behind their identity as God's people. Feelings of exile can help us to rediscover who we are. In the midst of exile we can ask, What can I learn about myself and about God in this situation?

God, I know you are with me, no matter what I feel.

Christian Humility

> Whoever becomes humble like this child is the
> greatest in the kingdom of heaven.
>
> (Matthew 18:4)

It is joyful to watch a child just being a child. Children who are not self-conscious sing for the pure joy of singing, dance in circles, and see their surroundings in awe and wonder. They are humble, and that is what Christ looks for in us. Arrogant people, the opposite of humble, are self-serving. They do things for their own gain, or for attention from others. These are not the qualities Christ points out as important. Christ wants us to know that humility and being childlike (not child*ish*) is part of his path. As we ask ourselves, Am I acting in humility or pride? we will know what we need to do to follow Christ. (And if we don't worry about what others think, we might have a little bit more fun doing it too!)

I present myself humbly to you, Lord Jesus, as a little child. Show me the way to your Kingdom.

God's Goodness

> Do not remember the sins of my youth or my
>   transgressions;
>   according to your steadfast love remember
>   me,
>   for your goodness' sake, O Lord!
>
> (Psalm 25:7)

We know people who remember everything, from what they wore last week to what we ate a year ago at a special restaurant. These memories are great when we are trying to recall something, but they can be a little annoying if our past mistakes are remembered as well. God doesn't hold on to the past. Once we have made our decision to live a life of faith, it doesn't mean we will never stumble or fall. It does mean, however, that we will do our best. When we don't, or cause hurt or harm, we seek forgiveness and resolve to make the future better. God doesn't hold on to our sins. He only remembers his own goodness and steadfast love.

O Lord, remember your steadfast love, and help me to remember it too.

Jesus Serves

> For the Son of Man came not to be served but to serve, and to give his life a ransom for many.
>
> (Mark 10:45)

Why do we serve? It helps to put service to others in the context of our faith tradition. Near the end of his earthly life, Jesus asked his followers to love one another. And so we serve one another out of love. We may start off by being required to do service for school or Confirmation preparation. The hope of our teachers and catechists is that, by doing required service, we develop an appreciation for Jesus' call to serve. As we are shown in the Gospels, Jesus never asked others to serve him. He served others. He gave us an example of service as he healed the sick, listened to those in need, and cared for those on the margins of society. When being called to do service, we can remind ourselves to ask, Am I doing this service as a response to Jesus and his mandate of love?

Jesus, you served others in love; may I respond by being a servant to those in need.

Pass On Cheerfulness

> Are any among you suffering? They should pray.
> Are any cheerful? They should sing songs of
> praise.
>
> (James 5:13)

It's nice to know that we are not just allowed but encouraged to express happiness. If our attitude is all gloom and doom, we aren't honoring the joy that God wants for us. We can follow God's ways and have fun too—and actually have more real fun if we are faith-filled. What could be more joyful than knowing we belong to God and are dearly loved? It's important for us to express that joy so others may come to know God as a God of love. Joy is infectious. If we are cheerful, we help others to become cheerful. When we pass on joy to others, they in turn pass it on to more people. Soon we've started a domino chain of happy, faith-filled people. So when we ask ourselves, How can I pass on God's love and joy to others? we can start with our own domino.

God of all joy, help me to know your love and joy deep in my heart, and to share it with others.

Integrity and Hope

> Is not your fear of God your confidence, and the
> integrity of your ways your hope?
>
> (Job 4:6)

We hope for things that we may have no control over. We do, however, have control over our integrity. We are the only ones who control it. If it is, as Job learns, a way to have hope, we can manage our integrity and enjoy the confidence hope brings. For Job endured many hardships and maintained his integrity through it all. As a result, he came through his trials and was rewarded for his faithfulness. Some ways to maintain our integrity include seeking advice before making decisions, making them with faith and confidence in God, and not changing who we are just to please others. We can start walking this road to hope by asking, What am I doing now that shows that I am a person of integrity?

Thank you, God, for helping me to follow your ways with integrity. Lead me along the road to hope.

True Love

> But the aim of such instruction is love that comes
> from a pure heart, a good conscience, and
> sincere faith.

> (1 Timothy 1:5)

According to advertising, wearing the "right" clothes, listening to the "right" music, or having the "right" stuff will bring love into our lives. But we know that material things are not love. But what is loving with a pure heart? It is loving with God's heart, with God's love. Loving with a pure heart leaves no room for impure motives, deceit, or self-serving manipulation. A good conscience and sincere faith support the love of a pure heart. But where do we learn about this love? We learn about it from instruction—from reading Scripture and other helpful books and learning about life and love from the best people we know. Taking the first step toward true love may mean asking ourselves, What is my image of love? and examining our answer closely.

God of true love, help me to love with a pure heart, a good conscience, and sincere faith.

Hitting Bottom

> Out of the depths I cry to you, O Lord.
> Lord, hear my voice!
>
> (Psalm 130:1–2)

When we hit bottom, or are in the depths, getting out seems nearly impossible. Our depths may come in the form of failing in school, losing friends, or having family problems. Being on the bottom feels like being lost in a deep, dark well. Is anyone up there? Can anyone hear me? These images really capture how we feel when we face difficult and painful circumstances. The psalmist prays a prayer that will work for us today. We cry out from the bottom, and no matter how far down we are, we don't have to worry about being heard. God hears us no matter how far down we are or what the situation is. When we are feeling low, at the very bottom, the following question may help us to focus: What do I need to talk to God about? We may also find God's guidance through confiding in a priest, religious sister, teacher, or school counselor.

O God, when I am in the depths, hear me and help me.

Genuine Popularity

> Let another praise you, and not your own mouth.
>
> (Proverbs 27:2)

When we become popular because others have noticed us and praised us, we have gained our popularity honestly. It is genuinely deserved, and our popularity can be a witness to our Gospel values. When we become popular because we brag about our accomplishments, our popularity will not last long. Having and keeping friends often means listening as well as talking. Though "tooting our own horn" is necessary at times (prospective colleges and employers, for example, want to know what we have accomplished), friends like us for who we are and not just for what we do. We also need to consider the source of others' popularity before becoming a fan. If others are genuine, and their ideals and actions are in alignment with Gospel values, we can certainly give them credit for that and join with them.

God, you love me for who I am and not for what I do. Thank you for true friends who do the same.

Alpha and Omega

> "I am the Alpha and the Omega, the first and the last, the beginning and the end."
>
> (Revelation 22:13)

In the Greek alphabet, Alpha is the first letter and Omega is the last letter. The symbols for them are A and Ω. These symbols can often be found in Christian art and architecture. Each year they are carved into the Paschal candle, a symbol of the Risen Christ. But what does it mean to say that Jesus is the beginning and the end? First of all, he is the beginning and the end of our lives. We come from God and, with faith in Jesus, we will go back to God. Or we can think of Jesus as the beginning and end of our faith story, or the beginning and end of all we need. It is comforting to know that Jesus is the beginning, the end, and everything in between. We might give some thought to this question, How can I honor Jesus as the Alpha and Omega of my life?

Jesus, Alpha and Omega of my life, guide me along the path of light and life, toward you.

Titus

> I left you behind in Crete for this reason, so that
> you should put in order what remained to be
> done, and should appoint elders in every town, as
> I directed you.
>
> (Titus 1:5)

From the time we are little children, we are asked, "What do you want to be when you grow up?" We give the usual answers: fireman, ballerina, or athlete. It is hard, though, to make choices as we grow older because the possibilities seem endless. Titus did not seem to have this problem because Paul recognized his gifts and talents. He saw Titus as a leader and guided him in his ministry. If we keep looking for direction in prayer to the Holy Spirit, if we keep listening to wise counsel from others, we will find our right path as well. In being aware of our gifts and talents, we too will be able to answer, What am I intended to do for God and others as I grow up?

Holy Spirit, amid the many choices before me, direct me in the right path for me.

Tools of Peace

> They shall beat their swords into plowshares,
>   and their spears into pruning hooks;
> nation shall not lift up sword against nation,
>   neither shall they learn war any more.

(Micah 4:3)

For some of us, war has taken place nearly our entire lives. Battlefields, bombs, and mourning for those killed in battle are realities that have accompanied our growing up. Yet we all seek a world of peace. Our ancestors in faith wanted peace too. They imagined a time when weapons would no longer be needed. Instruments of war could be reshaped into instruments of peace. (Plowshares and pruning hooks are farm tools.) We too can do the same thing. We can help to create peace by turning our own weapons—our negative words and actions—into words and actions of peace and justice. As we answer the question, What words and actions of mine need to be transformed? we do our part in shaping the peace we all seek.

Prince of Peace, help me to turn all my words and actions into tools of peace and justice.

Conserve and Protect

> As long as the earth endures,
>   seedtime and harvest, cold and heat,
> summer and winter, day and night,
>   shall not cease.

> (Genesis 8:22)

In creating the world, God gave us all we need to sustain life. After the Great Flood, God made a Covenant with Noah. God promised that the earth and its seasonal cycles would continue. In return, God requires an accounting for human life (see Genesis 9:5–6). We are now responsible for making sure that God's creation, including our environment and all of human life, is protected. How can we protect the environment and the human life that depends on it? We can help by reducing our carbon footprint; by keeping the oceans, lakes, and rivers free of pollutants; by reducing, reusing, recycling; by supporting clean air for everyone. When we ask ourselves, What actions can I take to conserve and protect the environment? we are taking the first step.

Creator God, thank you for our beautiful world. I will do my part to conserve and protect it.

Being Named

> And a voice came from heaven, "You are my Son, the Beloved; with you I am well pleased."
>
> (Mark 1:11)

When we were born, a voice told the hospital what name to put on our birth certificate. That same voice said our name during our Baptism when the priest asked. That voice (or voices) belonged to our parents, the ones who named us. Our families call us by name and our parents sometimes call us "Son" or "Daughter" to indicate that special relationship we share. God the Father called Jesus "Son" at his Baptism. Our identity is wrapped up in our name and our relationship with others. Our name also identifies us as beloved to God in Jesus Christ. We can reflect on the question, Who calls me by name, and how does that naming help to create my identity? knowing that first we belong to God.

Jesus, beloved Son of the Father, help me to appreciate being called Son or Daughter. Help me to never forget my identity as a child of God.

Kindness and Self-Esteem

> How can we thank God enough for you in
> return for all the joy that we feel before our God
> because of you?
>
> (1 Thessalonians 3:9)

We all have times of self-doubt, when self-esteem drags. At those times it seems hard to find ways to regain a healthy self-esteem or self-respect. We might not think of doing something for someone else as one way. However, when we do something nice or special for others, they often thank us. They let us know that we have made them happy. When we are appreciated, our self-esteem rises and it motivates us to do more for others. If we are lacking in self-esteem, it may be a good idea to look for ways to help or surprise someone else with an act of kindness. The road to better self-esteem may be in asking ourselves, Who could use a kind act or surprise from me?

God of surprises, show me ways to help others. Then surprise me with a renewed sense of self-worth!

Halloween

> To all God's beloved in Rome, who are called to
> be saints.
>
> (Romans 1:7)

As we prepare to celebrate All Saints' Day, we enjoy Halloween. The word *Halloween* is a shortened form of "All Hallows' Eve," the night before All Saints' Day. (*Hallow* means "holy," as in "hallowed be thy name.") In earlier times the night before All Saints' Day was a time of celebration and remembrance of all of those who have gone before us and who have died in the faith of Christ. We celebrate Halloween now with candy, costumes, and parties. Although most people do not grasp its religious significance, Halloween really is a victory celebration, for the saints are now victorious over sin, evil, and death. And we can do what they did. Each day we can look for ways to declare our own victory over evil, and ask: How can I choose good over evil today? How can I be a saint?

All the saints were followers who tried to do your will, Lord. Help me to choose good over evil every day, and celebrate my own victories in my heart.

All Saints' Day

Rejoice and be glad, for your reward is great in heaven.

(Matthew 5:12)

Today is All Saints' Day. Today we honor all the men and women who died in faith and who live with God in Heaven. Some we know by name; others are more obscure. Some are members of our own families. Each saint has his or her own unique story of following Christ. Saints come from all walks of life. They are married, single, priests, religious, men, women, and children. They are of all races and all nationalities. The saints remind us that becoming saints is our primary vocation in life: to open ourselves to God's love and extend it to others. And as we read in the lives of many saints, sometimes this kind of love takes great courage. Our journey in holiness began with Baptism. We can continue on the journey by asking ourselves: What am I doing today to open myself to God's love and extend it to others? What saint can I ask to help me?

Jesus, open me more and more to your love, and help me to share it with others.

All Souls' Day

> This is indeed the will of my Father, that all who
> see the Son and believe in him may have eternal
> life; and I will raise them up on the last day.
>
> (John 6:40)

Most of us know someone who has died, most likely someone from our own family. Emotions like anger and sadness are normal after a death and are part of a cycle that actually helps us to get through the grieving. Our faith tradition helps us as well. The vigil in prayer, along with a wake, a funeral, and special prayers at the graveside are examples of these traditions. After the funeral, pastoral care and counseling is often offered through the parish. On All Souls' Day, we remember all those who have died, especially those who are being purified in Purgatory. As we celebrate their lives, we can ask ourselves: Who has died that I knew and loved? How can I honor the memory of that special person?

Thank you, God, for the gift of the family and friends. Help us to remember that we, and our deceased loved ones, live in you.

Hosanna!

> So they took branches of palm trees and went out
> to meet him, shouting, "Hosanna! Blessed is the
> one who comes in the name of the Lord—the King
> of Israel!"

> (John 12:13)

Imagine being greeted like a rock star as we get out of
the car or bus at school! Was this how Jesus felt when he
was accepted so warmly by the crowds as he entered
Jerusalem? In any case, the enthusiasm of the people
did not last long. Sadly, this reflects our humanity in its
weakness. Sometimes we can start out enthusiastically
embracing an improvement in life—a resolution to be more
organized, to study harder, or to help out more at home or
school. Then, with one thing or another, we start slipping
back into our old habits. If we feel ourselves sliding back
into old habits of living, we can ask a friend to remind us
of our goals. We can ask: Am I doing what I said I would
do? Why not? And then we can begin again.

Jesus, be with me whenever I make a new decision or
begin a new way of doing things.

New Friends and Old

Do not abandon old friends,
for new ones cannot equal them.
A new friend is like new wine;
when it has aged, you can drink it with
pleasure.

(Sirach 9:10)

Wine connoisseurs tell us that the oldest wine is the best, and this biblical writer agrees. In today's terms the advice might read: "Do not dump your friends. New ones are good, but until you get to know and trust them, they can't equal tried and true friends." We might be tempted to dump or ignore our old friends when new ones come along. But we need to remember that our oldest friends are the ones who know us best, love us for who we are, and have even helped to shape our identity. Our oldest friends have brought us to where we are today. Before going off with new friends because of the excitement or popularity they offer, we can ask ourselves, Am I respecting my relationships with my oldest friends?

Jesus, you welcomed all friends, both old and new. Help me to do the same.

Advice to Ignore

Happy are those
who do not follow the advice of the wicked.

(Psalm 1:1)

We have all seen the results of someone (maybe even ourselves) following the advice of so-called friends. When these friends give advice that counters our faith and values, we recognize it as negative peer pressure. When we follow the advice of those who are not concerned with our best interests, the end result will not be a happy one. True happiness comes from not following bad advice or negative peer pressure. When making decisions, we need to try to predict consequences. When all is said and done, will we be saying, "I'm glad I did" or "I'm glad I didn't"? Thankfully we have a community that wants us to make decisions that bring life to ourselves and others. As we decide whose advice to follow, we can ask ourselves, Is this advice in alignment with my faith, my values, and my family's expectations of behavior?

Holy Spirit, guide me in all my decisions. Show me the way to true happiness.

Where Are You Now?

"Child, why have you treated us like this? Look, your father and I have been searching for you in great anxiety."

(Luke 3:48)

Jesus was young once, and this Gospel account is one that comforts many of us. He was doing something good, but he sort of got into trouble anyway. He didn't think Joseph and Mary should be getting upset. Sometimes we think we are doing the right thing too, but we end up in trouble. We might have gone to a friend's house to study and forgotten to tell our parents. Is that such a big deal? It is for our parents, who are left at home, thinking the worst. This Gospel account reminds us that we are called to honor our parents by keeping them informed. We owe it to our parents or other guardians to let them know where we are, what we are doing, and why. It may not seem important, but it is.

Jesus, your agenda did not always match Mary's and Joseph's, as mine does not always match that of my parents. Help us to keep our lines of communication open.

Self-Control

> And if anyone loves righteousness,
> her labors are virtues;
> for she teaches self-control and prudence,
> justice and courage;
> nothing in life is more profitable for mortals than
>   these.

> (Wisdom of Solomon 8:7)

Self-control, or temperance, is one of the four cardinal virtues, upon which all the other virtues depend. (The others are prudence, justice, and fortitude.) Self-control begins at an early age. Our parents teach us to control our tempers, to limit how much candy we eat, and to show care while playing with others. As we grow older, we are taught to control other aspects of our lives. The more we practice self-control, the stronger we will be. As we are faced with more choices, we can choose the ones that lead us to holiness, especially concerning intimacy with others. We can ask ourselves, How does the practice of self-control lead me to make good choices regarding physical intimacy?

Help me, Lord, to practice self-control, especially when facing choices regarding relationships and intimacy.

Strangers and Angels

> Do not neglect to show hospitality to strangers,
> for by doing that some have entertained angels
> without knowing it.
>
> (Hebrews 13:2)

The author of Hebrews is referring to Abraham's welcome to three strangers (see Genesis, chapter 18). It turned out that the strangers were messengers, or angels, from God. The Internet gives us many chances to welcome strangers, especially in posting comments. Positive or helpful comments make us God's good messengers. If our comments are negative or hurtful, we cross the line from posting to cyberbullying. The best practice with any online post is to read our comment and ask, If this were written to or about me, would I be okay with it? Remember that nothing on the Web ever goes away. Eventually, others—parents, college admissions officers, even future employers—may access it. On the Web, as everywhere else, our motto should be "best foot forward," or that foot could very well end up in mouth.

Holy Spirit, help me to be your messenger in all places, even on the Web.

God's Right Hand

Wondrously show your steadfast love,
 O savior of those who seek refuge
from their adversaries at your right hand.

(Psalm 17:7)

As little children, we may have grabbed on to our parent's leg or arm when we felt scared or shy. As we drove together in a car, a sudden stop meant that simultaneously a parent's right hand would shoot out in front of us, blocking potential harm. Even now, if we are watching a scary movie with a friend, we might grab that friend's arm as we scream out. We feel great comfort in knowing that a parent or friend is there for us in these moments. But greater than an arm to lean on at a movie is the right hand of God. That hand is there even if we don't reach out for it. Whatever happens, we are safe with God. We just need to ask, Can I reach out to God right now and seek refuge? When we do, the right hand of God is with us.

God of steadfast love, I seek refuge at your right hand.

Stopping Abuse

> For it is God's will that by doing right you should
> silence the ignorance of the foolish.
>
> (1 Peter 2:15)

People who abuse others typically do it out of fear or
ignorance. In order to silence them and to stop the abuse
or violence, we must be examples of God's goodness
and wisdom. God wants all of us to be happy, serving
one another and living justly. If we are an example of
this, we can help to silence those who are not. When we
encounter abuse or violence in our peers, it is God's will
that we help the victims (which may mean reporting abuse
or speaking out, without putting ourselves in danger) and,
by our own lives, show perpetrators the right way to live.
In encountering abuse, we can ask ourselves, How can
I do God's will in this situation? Reporting abuse and
speaking out, if possible, are acts of justice.

*God of compassion, abuse and violence are never
your will for us. Help me to do right by acting on the
side of justice.*

Selflessness

> So then, whenever we have an opportunity, let us work for the good of all, and especially for those of the family of faith.
>
> (Galatians 6:10)

If we are working for the good of all, it is hard to be selfish. As we learn what being a follower of Christ requires, we often hear about the value of selflessness. Christ was selfless when he preached the Kingdom of God, healed people, fed the hungry, and died on the cross for us. His sacrificial death is the ultimate example of selflessness. We participate in the death and Resurrection of Christ when we give of our time and talent to work for the good of all. Our faith calls us to die and rise in Christ. Through his grace and strength, especially in the Eucharist, we can answer the question, How can I work for the good of all as a living member of the Body of Christ?

Christ, you showed us the ultimate act of selflessness by your sacrifice on the cross. Help me to join with you in working for the good of all.

In the Name of the Lord

> And whatever you do, in word or deed, do
> everything in the name of the Lord Jesus, giving
> thanks to God the Father through him.
>
> (Colossians 3:17)

When we think about what doing something "in the name of" another, we realize the magnitude of that decision. Doing everything in the name of the Lord Jesus means that Jesus would approve of everything we do. It is easy to imagine doing service in the name of Jesus. But can we imagine dating in the name of Jesus? We know this would mean being honest and true to ourselves while bringing out the best in our date. It would also mean keeping pure sexually. If we are to date in the name of the Lord Jesus, we need support from family and friends, as well as from the person we are dating. We can learn if someone is right for us by asking ourselves, Will the person I'm dating honor the decisions I make in the name of Jesus?

Lord Jesus, help me to do everything in your name, including choosing the right persons to date.

A Whale of a Tale

> But Jonah set out to flee to Tarshish from the
> presence of the Lord.
>
> (Jonah 1:3)

When we do the exact opposite of what our parents or
teachers ask, we end up in trouble. Even if they never find
out, our conscience bothers us. When we do the exact
opposite of what God asks, the results are similar. This is
what we learn from the story of Jonah. This story is about a
prophet who was told by God to go and do one thing—
preach to the Ninevites—and who did the exact opposite.
He fled by ship, and, thrown into the sea by the crew,
was swallowed by a whale. The total isolation Jonah
experienced in the belly of the whale is our experience
when we do the opposite of what we are asked to do.
Once Jonah saw his mistake, he turned back to the path
God set for him. He knew that path would not be an easy
one, but he also knew that it was better than being stuck
in the belly of a whale!

*God, help me to hear your words and act on them.
Help me to follow the path you set for me.*

Generosity

> The miser is an evil person;
> he turns away and disregards people.

(Sirach 14:8)

The most well-known miser is a fictional character named Ebenezer Scrooge. Visited by the ghost of his former boss, Jacob Marley, Scrooge learned to be generous through dreams and nightmares. Scrooge's lesson is an example of Sirach's words above. Scrooge cared so much for his money that he turned away from the people who needed his help; he disregarded people and their needs. Scrooge was not just evil but very unhappy. When Scrooge learned to share and give to others, he not only turned away from evil, he gained a great deal more. His newfound connections to people made him happier than he had ever been. When we have money or other things to share, we can listen to Sirach, and, if we have been acting like Scrooge, we can always change our ways.

Good and generous God, help me to share what I have with others.

Active Waiting

> Be patient, therefore, beloved, until the coming of the Lord. The farmer waits for the precious crop from the earth, being patient with it until it receives the early and the late rains.

(James 5:7)

Studying is a lot like farming. Seeds are planted in students by teachers. Studying, doing homework, and taking notes are ways we care for the seeds planted in us. The hard part for many of us is being patient. We want to know what career we'll have, and what the seeds of our education will eventually produce. But, like the farmer and all those who wait for the coming of Christ, we must be patient. We show this patience by practicing "active waiting"—doing our part to care for and nurture the seeds of our faith and of our studies. Until the future becomes present to us, we can ask ourselves, In what areas of my faith life and school life do I need to practice patience?

Lord, help me to be both active and patient as I nurture the seeds of my education and my faith.

Negative Emotions

> Be angry but do not sin; do not let the sun go
> down on your anger.
>
> (Ephesians 4:26)

Feelings are not sins because they are not choices. We should listen to feelings and learn from them, but we cannot let them take over our decision-making power—that is, our thoughts and our choices. If we are overwhelmed by negative feelings (anger, revenge, resentment), we can choose to change our feelings by changing our thinking. New information, for example, can lead to new thoughts, which can lead to different feelings. This Scripture verse reminds us that our emotions are valid, and that they are not wrong in themselves. But we do need to confront them with our thoughts, and then make good decisions. So if we are angry, we can examine the reason for that feeling and ask ourselves: What can I learn from this feeling? What do I know or need to find out to change or influence my thinking?

Lord, help me when I am overwhelmed with negative emotions. Thank you for my power to feel, to think, and to choose.

Obey the Lord

All these blessings shall come upon you and overtake you, if you obey the Lord your God.

(Deuteronomy 28:2)

A commitment is often a two-way agreement. If one person does *X*, the other will do *Y*. If we work a certain number of hours, we get paid a dollar amount. If we do part of a class project, our partner will do another part. The commitments we make to God are also reciprocal. If we follow God's commands, we will have blessings. What kind of blessings? This doesn't mean we will be given large sums of money, perfect health, or continual happiness. It does mean that we will know the presence, strength, and love of God in our lives. When we decide to say yes to the question, Will I make a commitment to follow God's ways? we know there will be blessings.

God of all blessings, I commit myself to your ways. May I know your presence, your strength, and your love in my life.

Light of Christ

> This is the message we have heard from him and proclaim to you, that God is light and in him there is no darkness at all.
>
> (1 John 1:5)

Being afraid of the dark is common. When the lights go out, there is a sense of the unknown and unseen, which is unsettling. Little children (and even some adults) sleep with night lights to ward off that fear. The fear of life without Christ is similar to fear of the dark. A life without Christ is filled with unknown and unsettling moments. Although we have no crystal ball to see the future, a Christian life is a life with a crystal clear future. Our future is filled with light, the light of love and joy. We can be reminded of that light-filled future when we ask Christ, the Light, to come into our lives. At the end of every day, we can ask ourselves, When and where did I see Christ's light today? before turning off our bedroom lights.

Jesus, you are our light and our life. Thank you for the crystal clear future you offer to me.

Eternal Life

Whoever believes in the Son has eternal life.

(John 3:36)

As we grow up, we realize that most decisions have both challenges and rewards. The decision to be on a team means the challenge of teamwork and the reward of shared victory. Being Christian has its challenges and rewards too. As Christians we face the challenges of following Jesus, loving one another, living a moral life, being of service to others, and doing all in Jesus' name. The rewards in the Christian life are called "the fruits of the Holy Spirit": joy, peace, and love are among them. In addition, in John's Gospel we are promised a very big reward: eternal life. This reward may seem remote, but it will mean more to us as people we love pass from this life to the next. Even now, as we face the challenges of our faith, we can reflect on that reward and ask, Am I making a decision that I will be proud of for all eternity?

Jesus, help me to remember the promise of eternal life as I face the challenges of following you.

Examination of Conscience

> Examine yourselves to see whether you are living in the faith. Test yourselves.
>
> (2 Corinthians 13:5)

There is a practice called examination of conscience that we as Catholics practice as we prepare for Reconciliation. Some of us do this in a group setting at a special service, and others do this as we individually prepare for the Sacrament. Most of the time in the practice, we read and reflect on the Ten Commandments and think about how well we have kept them. If we take the time to practice and make an examination of conscience, we can be more fully prepared to participate in the Sacrament of Reconciliation and to seek forgiveness in our daily lives. By asking ourselves, Have I examined myself lately and tested how well I am living out my faith? we will know if it is time for us to seek forgiveness from God and others.

As I examine myself against your commandments, God, I pray that I seek and give forgiveness freely.

An Attitude of Gratitude

Praise the Lord!
O give thanks to the Lord, for he is good;
for his steadfast love endures forever.

(Psalm 106:1)

As Thanksgiving Day approaches, it is a good time to get in touch with our American roots. Although Thanksgiving Day is a secular holiday, it has its roots in the virtue of gratitude. Faced with the possibility of starvation, the pilgrims gratefully accepted help from their Native American neighbors, and, in turn, invited them to their harvest feast. When we celebrate Thanksgiving, we can remember that the foundation stones of our country were set on gratitude and harmony. We still need to live these attitudes in our country today—in our families, in our schools, and in our government. And every day we can ask ourselves, How can I live out my gratitude to God and my harmony with others today?

God, we thank you for all your blessings. Help us to share them with others in an attitude of gratitude and harmony.

Serving the Lord Together

> But as for me and my household, we will serve the Lord.
>
> (Joshua 24:15)

Each of our families has a unique way of serving the Lord. Some households serve Jesus in others by making meals for the homeless or volunteering at a senior center. Some households donate extra clothing and other items to a local charity. Others help at Mass on Sundays as lectors, altar servers, or choir members. If we take the time to reflect as a family on ways to serve the Lord, we can personalize our effort. A family that appreciates the outdoors can serve by helping to protect the environment in some way. Another family with creative gifts can serve by decorating the church at special seasons of the year. By asking our family, "What are our family's gifts and how can we use them to serve the Lord together?" we can start the conversation.

Lord, I want to serve you. Help our whole family find a way to share our gifts in service.

The Heart's Desires

Take delight in the Lord,
and he will give you the desires of your heart.

(Psalm 37:4)

If we are happy in the Lord, God will give us the desires of our heart. This seems like a pretty quick path to getting what we want. But if we have desires that are counter to God's ways, they cannot be of the heart; they will be purely selfish, of the flesh or of the world. A desire of our heart implies that it is residing in the same place God resides. Therefore God and something ungodly cannot coexist in the same place. Practically speaking, what does this mean? First, we must trust God's providence for us, and find the goodness in what God provides. Second, we must test our own heart. This may sound hard to do. However, it is not really difficult to determine a true desire of the heart when we ask ourselves, Can God and this desire both reside in my heart?

God, you know my heart. Help me to test my heart, and reject all that is not of you.

Hope in Suffering

> If, in fact, we suffer with him so that we may also be glorified with him.

> (Romans 8:17)

"There is light at the end of the tunnel." We hear this from friends and family when we are going through a hard time. They help us to see the positive side of things or at least help us to realize that our troubles won't last forever. In hard times, we need words of hope. Paul provides these words of hope to the Romans and therefore to all of us as we experience difficulties in life. He reminds us of Christ's death but also of his Resurrection. He reminds us that Christ suffered for us and also brought us the hope of new life. These comforting words helped the Romans in hard times, and they provide the same comfort to us. By asking ourselves, Where is my ultimate and lasting hope? we are able to see that Christ is the light at the end of the tunnel.

Lord of hope, help me to see your light at the end of the tunnel, especially in hard times.

Beloved

> Beloved, let us love one another, because love is from God; everyone who loves is born of God and knows God.
>
> (1 John 4:7)

Throughout the New Testament, we read the word *beloved* as an address to the early Christians. It may sound old-fashioned to us, and we probably wouldn't use it to address our family and friends. However, if we reflect on what the word *beloved* means, we may want to at least think about it before speaking to those who are close to us. *Beloved* means "dearly loved." How would we follow up a greeting if we start it with "Beloved"? Would we be able to yell at our little brother or sister after calling him or her beloved? Would we be able to ignore our parents as they call us beloved? Would we be able to be mean to a classmate or teacher if we addressed them with this title?

Lord, you love me and call me beloved. May I see others as dearly loved before speaking or reacting to them.

Compassion

Moved with compassion, Jesus touched their eyes. Immediately they regained their sight and followed him.

(Matthew 20:34)

Suffering is all around us. Sometimes it is obvious—a blind person negotiates a crowded sidewalk with a special stick or a seeing-eye dog, a homeless man begs for money on the street, a family lives in a shelter because they have no permanent home. Jesus met the suffering he saw with compassion. We are asked to do the same. We share in Christ's compassion when we help others. We also share when we accept help; by letting others help us, we allow them to share in Christ's compassion. Learning to be both the giver and receiver of help is part of growing in our faith. If we suffer, we might ask, Who has offered to help me; am I ready to accept their help? As we approach others who are suffering, we can ask, How can I share in Christ's compassion for this person?

Compassionate Christ, help me to extend your compassion to others and to accept it when I am in need.

Harmony

> Live in harmony with one another; do not be
> haughty, but associate with the lowly; do not claim
> to be wiser than you are.

> (Romans 12:16)

By acting haughty we may think we will gain popularity, hoping others might see us as important. We may hope to be invited to join the more popular groups. However, this plan may backfire, as people tend to distrust those who are two-faced and claim to be something they are not. In contrast, we are called to live in harmony, to associate with all, and to be humble. Humility is the opposite of haughtiness. We find that the call to follow Christ in faith may not be easy, but humility, honesty, and acceptance will eventually lead us to true friends. Being true to who we are and what we are called to do require us to reflect on the question, How do I contribute to harmony through my humility, honesty, and acceptance of others?

*God of harmony and acceptance, help me to follow
your ways and find true friends.*

Messiah

> But these are written so that you may come to
> believe that Jesus is the Messiah, the Son of God,
> and that through believing you may have life in his
> name.

> (John 20:31)

Jesus is both human and divine; he was born of a woman,
breathed, ate, wept, and died. He also is divine. As the
Second Person of the Blessed Trinity, he is one with God
the Father and the Holy Spirit from all eternity, and was
raised from the dead. Because Jesus is both man and
God, we recognize him as one of us while at the same
time worship him as God. The name Jesus is worthy of
honor, and it is a Catholic custom to bow the head when
saying or hearing the name of Jesus. We know Jesus by
a variety of other names: the Word of God, Christ, the
Anointed One, the Messiah. Each of these names reflects,
in some way, who Jesus is to us. When we address Jesus,
it is important to remember to ask ourselves, Am I honoring
Jesus by using his name with reverence?

*Jesus, Messiah, Anointed One, may I do everything
in your name.*

Continue in Jesus' Word

> Then Jesus said to the Jews who had believed in him, "If you continue in my word, you are truly my disciples."

> (John 8:31)

When we want to know how to do something, we need to find the best person to tell us. The best person is usually not a peer or coworker. Although they may want to help us, they may have only a secondhand answer or a personal opinion. If we want the absolute answer, we go to the leader. By going straight to the best person, the expert or head, we avoid the uncertainty that goes with secondhand information. Jesus is our leader, and he tells us exactly what we need to do. Because we are called to be his followers, we learn that we must continue in his Word. What Jesus doesn't tell us directly is how we are going to do that. As we grow in age and faith and maturity, we will discern answers. Until then, we can reflect on this question, How am I continuing in Jesus' word?

Thank you, Jesus, for the answer to what I need to do. Help me to discern the best way to do it.

Proclaim Peace and Justice

> Look! On the mountains the feet of one who brings
> good tidings, who proclaims peace!
>
> (Nahum 1:15)

When we bring good news to people, they hug us or thank us; it's great to be a messenger of peace and happiness. The Prophet Nahum reminds us that those who announce peace and justice are always welcomed. We can be that messenger each time we bring peace and justice to others. People all around the world are waiting for the good news of peace and justice. We can help bring good tidings to them by participating in works of advocacy. We can participate in letter-writing campaigns, awareness programs, and peaceful protests against injustices. We can also proclaim peace in our own lives when we reflect on the question, What can I change in my own life to be a more just and peaceful person?

God of peace and justice, help me to look at my own life and then find ways to bring peace and justice to others.

We Shine Like Stars

> Be blameless and innocent, children of God
> without blemish in the midst of a crooked and
> perverse generation, in which you shine like stars
> in the world.
>
> (Philippians 2:15)

Every day we use labels to identify ourselves. Sometimes these labels describe what we do or enjoy: athlete, scholar, artist, sports fan, geek. Other times we describe ourselves by ethnicity, gender, or culture. Our labels often highlight what makes us unique as individuals, but the Letter to the Philippians calls us to embrace an important label that unites us with one another: "children of God." The responsibilities of this common identity have been explained throughout Scripture and Church teaching. The Letter to the Philippians challenges us, as children of God, to shine as stars or lights in the world. In this season when we light candles for Advent, how do you, as a child of God, shine like a light for others?

Jesus, as we wait for your coming at Christmas, may I too embrace my true identity as a child of God and be a light for others.

Self-Esteem and Humility

> For we are what he has made us, created in
> Christ Jesus for good works, which God prepared
> beforehand to be our way of life.
>
> (Ephesians 2:10)

We often base our self-esteem on how we look or how we do in school or activities. Positive or negative feedback about our appearance, intelligence, or ability can affect how we feel about ourselves and our worth. When we become too focused on success and others' praise, we can swing between extremes of liking and disliking ourselves. So how do we keep our self-esteem in balance—recognizing and valuing our God-given worth without getting too full of ourselves? We can do this by remembering that each of us is created in Christ Jesus. Our faith helps us to understand that God is our way of life, that we can do nothing without him, and that everything we do is for him. Knowing that you are of God and for God, how does the way you feel about yourself reflect your faith?

Christ Jesus, may I learn to balance my self-esteem with humility as a reflection of my faith and love for you.

Honor the Maker

Those who oppress the poor insult their Maker,
but those who are kind to the needy honor
him.

(Proverbs 14:31)

One way to honor someone we love and respect is to do something in his or her name. For example, to honor loved ones who have died, families sometimes create scholarship funds in their name. Sometimes athletes or artists dedicate their efforts to someone special. So how can we honor God and show him our love and respect? We honor him by reflecting our faith in what we say, do, and think. Accepting others is one important way we can show honor to God, for he calls us to show kindness to those in need. And not all needs are obvious. Do you know anyone who needs acceptance and friendship? Consider who you have accepted into your circle of friends—and who you have not. We can ask ourselves, Am I honoring God in the way I treat my peers?

Creator God, maker of all, may I welcome all who need acceptance and love.

Sharing the Good News

> And why has this happened to me, that the mother of my Lord comes to me?
>
> (Luke 1:43)

Elizabeth was probably surprised by Mary's visit. But as soon as Elizabeth heard Mary, she knew that something special was happening. The baby Elizabeth was carrying leapt in her womb and, filled with the Holy Spirit, Elizabeth greeted Mary by saying, "Blessed are you among women, and blessed is the fruit of your womb" (Luke 1:42). Excited to see her friend and cousin, Elizabeth knew that Mary had good news even before they had a conversation. Our visits to our friends can be filled with the same joy and excitement when we bring the Good News with us. Mary brought the Good News in the form of the baby Jesus. How can you share it in your words and actions?

Jesus, help me to honor you and bring your Good News to all my friends, just as your mother, Mary, shared the Good News with Elizabeth.

We Choose for Ourselves

Do not say, "It was he who led me astray";
for he has no need of the sinful.

(Sirach 15:12)

Have you ever done something sinful or harmful just to be part of the crowd? When our friends are doing something we know is wrong—such as cheating on a test or bullying someone—it can be hard not to go along. If we give in, we may find it easy to blame everyone else. Maybe we even blame God for allowing us to take part. However, we must remember that God created us with free will, because he wants us to freely choose to love and serve him. The freedom to make our own decisions means that the responsibility for choosing between right and wrong is ours alone. The next time we face a difficult choice, we can stop and ask ourselves: Is this something wrong that I will later blame on others or on God? Or am I choosing to do this because I know it is the right thing to do?

God, you have no use for the sinful, and neither do I. Grant me the strength to see and choose what is right, even if it is not the popular choice.

Wise Children

A wise child makes a glad father,
but a foolish child is a mother's grief.

(Proverbs 10:1)

As we make our own decisions and describe them to our parents, their response helps us to know how they feel. When we tell them about studying for a hard test instead of hanging out with our friends, our parents are happy. When we tell them about getting in trouble, they worry. We honor our parents in many ways; one way is to demonstrate how well we've learned the wisdom of what they've taught us. It takes time to grow in wisdom. But as we apply the lessons of our faith and family, we see how they pay off. Wisdom is not about grades or external measures of success. Rather, it is reflected in how we make decisions, what we do with our spare time, and how we interact with others. As we make decisions today, we can demonstrate wisdom by asking ourselves, Would this decision make my parents glad or cause them grief?

God, help me to learn wisdom so I can make decisions that honor my parents and you.

Obeying Passions?

> Therefore, do not let sin exercise dominion in your mortal bodies, to make you obey their passions.
>
> (Romans 6:12)

Obeying our passions—doesn't that sound like fun? We'd eat junk food all day, skip class when we felt like it, and pursue any pleasure whenever we want. But we know there are consequences, like making ourselves sick or overweight or falling behind in school. We can expect spiritual and emotional consequences as well. We are called to respect our mind and body as God's temple. Recklessly giving in to the passions of our mortal bodies does not respect God's image in us. Instead of feeling fulfilled, we may feel empty and used. Our faith teaches us that we are called not to follow our passions blindly but rather to listen to the guidance of the Holy Spirit. The next time we encounter temptation, we can ask, What will support my long-term good and honor God?

God, I sometimes desire things that I know are not part of your plan for me. Help me to keep your ways and stay on your path.

Talking to Bullies

> Jesus answered, "If I have spoken wrongly, testify to the wrong. But if I have spoken rightly, why do you strike me?"
>
> (John 18:23)

Jesus dealt with his share of bullies, and we can follow his example when someone is bullying us. For example, we can try to walk away, ignore the bully, or simply refuse to respond—reflecting mercy, as Jesus advised when he told us to turn the other cheek (see Matthew 5:39). Or we can try to talk to the bully, as Jesus did on many occasions when others challenged him or those around him. If someone is bullying you, consider asking the bully why he or she is acting this way. This question may invite the person to pause and reflect. Even if trying to communicate does not completely stop the bullying, you may create a space that allows both you and the bully to slow down. You may even get an answer that surprises you and opens the possibility of reconciliation.

Christ Jesus, in your life and Passion, you showed us how to talk to bullies. Help me respond to bullies as you would.

Calm in the Storm

> They went to him and woke him up, shouting, "Master, Master, we are perishing!" And he woke up and rebuked the wind and the raging waves; they ceased, and there was a calm.
>
> (Luke 8:24)

When we call 911 in an emergency, we expect to receive help fairly quickly. When we go to a school counselor, we also get help. However, sometimes we need help and comfort that only God can provide. In those times all we need to do is pray. In Luke's Gospel we hear how Jesus calmed a storm and helped his disciples feel safe. When we experience a trying time, we can ask ourselves, How can my faith help me to get through this situation?

Christ who calms the sea, help me during the storms in my own life. May I remember to call on you for aid in times of trouble.

How to Respond?

> And we urge you, beloved, to admonish the
> idlers, encourage the fainthearted, help the weak,
> be patient with all of them.
>
> (1 Thessalonians 5:14)

When we witness one young person fighting with or bullying another, we are called to respond in a faithful way. However, it can be difficult to know what to do. In these final words to the Thessalonians, Paul is encouraging the community to help one another and support one another in faith and love. If we take our role as community members seriously, we understand that we can't ignore violence when we see it. We must constantly encourage others to be their best and to behave in ways that reflect the faith we claim. When we are confronted with violence, or when we witness violence occurring in the lives of others, we can ask: What is the best way to actively respond to this situation that does not endanger myself? How can I continually help to build a community of faith and love?"

God, as I learn your ways, help me to respond in a faith-filled way to violent and abusive situations I may witness.

Integrity

> I will study the way that is blameless.
>> When shall I attain it?
>
> I will walk with integrity of heart within my house.
>
> (Psalm 101:2)

We know our faith includes certain values. Some are easy to identify, such as the commandments to love God above everything and our neighbor as ourselves. But some of our values may take us longer to identify. The psalmist reminds us that it takes time to learn everything about our faith. It is comforting to know that having faith does not mean we have to know everything. In fact, learning about our faith is part of our tradition. As long as we proceed with integrity, we can work toward learning the way that is blameless. Integrity is a quality of total honesty and consistency in our approach to ourselves, one another, and God. We will make mistakes—but with integrity as our guiding principle, we will learn the ways of our faith and grow in our ability to live by its values.

God, I long to walk as a blameless follower, but I know I have a lot to learn. Teach me integrity as I seek to follow you.

Living Freedom Wisely

> For you were called to freedom, brothers and
> sisters; only do not use your freedom as an
> opportunity for self-indulgence.
>
> (Galatians 5:13)

Some parents have strict rules governing when, how, and whom their children can date. These ground rules are appropriate for our safety and support as we learn to develop mature adult relationships. Still, for the most part, we choose for ourselves the people we date. But this does not mean we can do whatever we wish with whomever we wish. As with everything in a Christian's life, dating is an opportunity to practice how to live faithfully. The love and respect we are called to have for all people and the freedom we are called to use wisely applies to all areas of our lives. When you go on a date, ask yourself, Am I abusing or embracing the freedom God has given me?

Christ Jesus, you call me to follow you in all moments of my life, even dating. Grant me the wisdom I need to develop healthy relationships.

Walk in Faith

For we walk by faith, not by sight.

(2 Corinthians 5:7)

Have you ever witnessed or even experienced a faith walk? A faith walk is an exercise in which one person who is blindfolded is guided along a path by someone who can see. Through this experience we can begin to understand how relying on another person—trusting that he or she will not lead us astray—can help us to grow in our faith life, teaching us how to rely on God even though we cannot see him. He calls us to have faith in him and in our family, church, and community. As we mature as faithful believers, we learn that we will never be able to see God or fully know his plan for us. We experience his guidance, however, when we allow ourselves to walk in faith. We can practice this skill in any situation by asking ourselves, How can I walk in faith in this moment?

God, I do have faith in you. I will practice walking in faith.

Eternal Riches

As for those who in the present age are rich,
command them not to be haughty, or to set their
hopes on the uncertainty of riches, but rather on
God who richly provides us with everything for our
enjoyment.

(1 Timothy 6:17)

Material comfort is not wrong, but we are called as
Christians to use our earthly goods to serve God and to
help those less fortunate, knowing that the more we have,
the more difficult we may find this call. In his First Letter
to Timothy, Paul reminds us that earthly riches don't make
us better than others, and good fortune today may not
continue tomorrow. Instead he calls us to look forward to
the riches of Heaven. Are you striving toward the riches of
this world or those of the next?

*Father, you provide what we need to be healthy and
safe. Help us to serve others in need and to work
toward the riches of eternal life with you.*

Divine Wisdom

But the wisdom from above is first pure, then peaceable, gentle, willing to yield, full of mercy and good fruits, without a trace of partiality or hypocrisy.

(James 3:17)

We know that study and hard work help us to grow in academic ability and knowledge. At the same time, we must also work to develop wisdom, particularly wisdom from above. What helps us to become more wise? We can study Scripture and Tradition, celebrate the Sacraments, and actively participate in our church community. The academic abilities we develop will help us in college and in an eventual career, but divine wisdom is what helps us to follow the path of faith as we make decisions, form relationships, and face the ups and downs of life. As we study for school, we can ask ourselves, What am I doing to develop the wisdom I need to go through life as a faithful Christian?

God of all knowledge, thank you for the opportunities I have through education. Help me also to appreciate and develop the wisdom that I can find only in you.

Unjust Anger

Unjust anger cannot be justified,
for anger tips the scale to one's ruin.

(Sirach 1:22)

Getting upset over small stuff and taking things personally can tempt us into unjust anger. It is unjust to get angry at something uncontrollable, like traffic, or something trivial, like spilling juice. When we are feeling insecure, we might become unjustly angry with another person, such as a classmate who gets a better grade. When we give in to unjust anger, and especially when we turn our anger on people unfairly, we set ourselves on a path toward injustice in other areas. On this path we can lose sight of what is important in this life and forget the promise of Heaven in the next. The next time we feel ourselves getting angry, we can ask: Is this anger just or unjust? If it is unjust, how can I replace it with patience and acceptance?

God of compassion, I know it is okay to get angry. Help me to learn when anger is justified, and grant me the patience to let go of unjust anger, so that I may stay on the path of faith.

A Commitment to Keep

All this took place to fulfill what had been spoken by the Lord through the prophet: "Look, the virgin shall conceive and bear a son, and they shall name him Emmanuel," which means, "God is with us."

(Matthew 1:22–23)

God made a lot of promises in the Old Testament, didn't he? Of the commitments God kept, the most important was the promise of the Messiah. Mary's yes made it possible for God the Father to fulfill this promise in Jesus' birth. In the last week before Christmas, look at your own commitments. How can you fulfill the commitments that are good and faithful? If you have made promises that are not consistent with a faith-filled life, how can you let those go? When we take time during Advent to consider which commitments to reaffirm and which to let go, we honor God's commitment and Mary's yes.

Emmanuel, help me say yes to those commitments that bring me closer to you. Grant me the wisdom to identify and give up those commitments that are not part of your plan.

God Hears

In my distress I called upon the Lord;
  to my God I called.
From his temple he heard my voice,
  and my cry came to his ears.

(2 Samuel 22:7)

Friends know us by our laughs. Parents know us by the way we say "Mom" or "Dad." Even our pets recognize us when we call them. Is it surprising, then, to be told that God hears us in our distress? He knows our voices—he hears our cries for help and comfort even when we don't say a word. He doesn't always answer our prayers in the way we hope, but we know that he hears us, shares our pain, and has a plan for us that will become clear in time. In any moment of fear, sorrow, or distress, we just need to call on God, out loud or in our heart, and know we are heard. How can this confidence fill you with courage? How does it help you to continue in faith, even in times of suffering?

Father, I know you hear me, even when my heart and not my voice cries out to you. Thank you for the courage and strength you provide. Grant me the patience to know you have a plan for me.

Myths and Superstitions

> Have nothing to do with profane myths and old wives' tales. Train yourself in godliness.
>
> (1 Timothy 4:7)

Avoiding a sidewalk crack or a black cat is a relatively harmless impulse. Superstitions are partly about fun and partly about tradition. However, if we begin to embrace such beliefs and myths as truth, taking them so seriously that they cloud our understanding, we endanger our ability to respond to our call to holiness. We must recognize when false beliefs get in the way of our faith, and leave space for the important truths of our faith to shine through. Are we following superstitions that prevent us from growing in faith and godliness?

God, only you are the way to a faith-filled life. Help me to avoid superstitions that make it difficult for me to grow in true faith in you.

The Path of Forgiveness

> Although you are sovereign in strength, you judge
> with mildness,
> and with great forbearance you govern us;
> for you have power to act whenever you choose.
>
> (Wisdom of Solomon 12:18)

Have you ever put off telling your teacher or parents about a mistake you made? The time between making a mistake and telling a teacher or parent can be worse than the punishment. We imagine the trouble we'll be in. But unless our mistake was really terrible, the actual consequences are often less than we fear. In the end, our teachers and parents have our best interests at heart and want to help us mature into wise, good adults. God is that way too. He forgives easily and judges us mildly. Whether we fear going to God or to our parents or teachers, we can ask ourselves what is worse: our internal fear and judgment, or the relief of telling the truth and being forgiven.

God of mild judgment, help me to be truthful with you, my parents, and teachers, and to ask for forgiveness when I have wronged others.

Sharing as Service

> Give some of your food to the hungry, and some
> of your clothing to the naked. Give all your surplus
> as alms, and do not let your eye begrudge your
> giving of alms.

(Tobit 4:16)

We serve others most directly when we give food,
clothing, and other resources. Hungry people need food.
People with little to wear need clothing. Those who are
poor need help to provide the basic necessities of life for
themselves and their families. Advent and Christmas are
the perfect time to go through closets for clothing to donate,
buy extra canned goods for food drives, and share our
holiday money with others. The Book of Tobit tells us not
to begrudge these offerings. Instead, when we share our
goods with those less fortunate, we are called to do so
with joy. Think of the joy you will experience when you
exchange presents with loved ones on Christmas. How
can you extend this joy to sharing with those in need?

*God of all that is good, help me to freely share what
I have.*

United in Love

> I want their hearts to be encouraged and united
> in love, so that they may have all the riches of
> assured understanding and have the knowledge of
> God's mystery, that is, Christ himself.
>
> (Colossians 2:2)

Imagine writing your Christmas list with "Christ," "peace," and "love" as your top three items. Indeed, when we stop thinking of the material things we want and instead focus on what we need, we might find that Christ, peace, and love are our top requests. Placing them first in our heart encourages us to focus on building the Kingdom of God. We prepare for Christ's coming during Advent especially, but how can we make it a priority all year? In these final days before we celebrate the birth of Christ once more, how can you unite with others in love and welcome Christ now and all year long?

Christ Jesus, as we prepare to celebrate your birth, help me to keep you and the promises of your love and unity as my top priorities—now and throughout the year.

Peace Crushes Evil

> The God of peace will shortly crush Satan under your feet. The grace of our Lord Jesus Christ be with you.
>
> (Romans 16:20)

One of our hopes as God's faithful people is to overcome Satan's power. We put this hope into action by bringing a spirit of love and peace into everything we do. By doing the opposite of what Satan wants, we help to crush evil. Keeping the grace of Jesus Christ with us strengthens our ability to avoid temptation and instead work toward peace and justice. Christ's coming at Christmas reminds us to work even harder to help stamp out evil. As we finish our holiday preparations, we can ask ourselves what we can do today to help peace and love flourish.

Father, help me to take actions that bring your peace and love to others.

Owe Love Only

> Owe no one anything, except to love one another; for the one who loves another has fulfilled the law.
>
> (Romans 13:8)

Today is a great day to wipe all debts clean and to owe and expect only love. If someone owes us a favor or a small sum of money, we can forgive that debt and ask him or her to repay with love instead. If we owe someone else, we can pay our debts and add love on top. As we get ready to spend time with loved ones on this final day before Christmas, we are called to remember that true fulfillment lies in focusing on what we can give, not on what we expect to receive. No matter how much money we have, how late a store is open, or whether we have time to shop, we can always give love. Before the excitement of Christmas tomorrow, take some time to reflect. How can we spread love today and throughout the year?

God of love, I long to fulfill your law. Help me to live a faithful life by sharing your love with others.

Celebrating Christmas

> And [Mary] gave birth to her firstborn son and wrapped him in bands of cloth, and laid him in a manger.
>
> (Luke 2:7)

We have much to celebrate today. We rejoice in Mary's yes, Joseph's faithfulness, the fulfillment of ancient prophecies, the birth of our Savior, and of course the love of friends and family. Christmas provides us with an opportunity to celebrate all these good things with loved ones and to praise God and welcome Christ again. Amid all the fun and festivities of the day, make time to reflect on this question: As I celebrate today, how can I show the true meaning of Christmas to all I meet?

Jesus, son of Mary and adopted son of Joseph, today I praise you and thank you for all the good you have done for me and through me, this year and always.

Sharing Suffering

> When Jesus saw his mother and the disciple
> whom he loved standing beside her, he said to his
> mother, "Woman, here is your son." Then he said
> to the disciple, "Here is your mother."
>
> (John 19:26–27)

Being a family means sharing suffering as well as joy.
We know that Jesus suffered at his Crucifixion—but what
about those who loved him? His mother and the Beloved
Disciple were there. Can you imagine how much your
family and friends would grieve if they had to watch you
going through such torment? Christ gave his loved ones
relief even in his last moments by bestowing the gift of
family on them. Mary must have found some comfort in
being called "Mother" by the disciple her son loved, just
as the disciple took comfort in being called "Son" by the
mother of Jesus. Do you know anyone who is suffering?
How can you share their suffering and be family to them
in their time of need?

*Jesus, by your suffering you saved me. Thank you
for your gift of redemption, and help me to ease the
suffering of others by sharing their burden.*

Upside-Down Popularity

> "Whoever welcomes this child in my name welcomes me, and whoever welcomes me welcomes the one who sent me; for the least among all of you is the greatest."
>
> (Luke 9:48)

Envision coming to school one day and finding the least popular kid has become the most popular overnight. Can you imagine the surprise and bewilderment? Likewise, in a time of strict cultural and socioeconomic divisions, the early followers of Jesus must have been astonished when he stated that the least were in fact the greatest. We know that Christ often offered guidance that turned his listeners' expectations and customs upside-down. We can continue Christ's work today by treating the "lowliest" among us with kindness and respect, even when it runs against the norm. Who in your school or community should be raised up? You can help reverse the popular notion of greatness by looking for the image of God in everyone.

Christ, you turned popularity upside-down. Help me to see you in everyone I encounter, from the greatest to the most lowly.

Risen Christ

He is not here; for he has been raised.

(Matthew 28:6)

Throughout Scripture, we find descriptions of the Holy Trinity that help us to develop a relationship with God. In particular, our experience of God through the Risen Christ provides as much hope now as it did in the days following Jesus' death. Knowing that he rose again after dying on the cross provided the early Christians with the strength and courage to continue on the path Jesus laid out. Likewise, calling to mind an image of the Risen Christ, radiating peace and love as he reaches out to us, can comfort us in times of need and expand our joy when things go well. As we close this year and continue the celebration of Christ's birth, we reflect on the reason God sent his only Son. How can the image of the Risen Christ provide us with the greatest hope, comfort, and joy?

God, you answer to many titles, but all point the way to you. Help me to know you through the life, death, and Resurrection of your Son, and grant me the wisdom to turn to you in times of joy as well as need.

I Will Follow You

"Follow me."
(Luke 5:27)

Just as he called the tax collector, Jesus calls all of us today: "Follow me." Sometimes we may want to say, "Later, not now." Other times we may not want to hear it at all, saying: "It's too difficult. It requires too much." Whether we choose to embrace this call or put it off, we know that our call to follow Christ began with our Baptism, which washed away Original Sin and granted us the grace we need to find our way to him. Even when we say yes eagerly and joyfully, we may not know how Christ wants us to follow him in a given moment. The important thing is that we take time to learn what it means to follow him and to believe that he will call us only for good. What do you think Jesus is calling you to do? Who can you ask to help you discern the answer to this question?

Jesus, I know you are asking me to follow you. Help me to learn what it is you want me to do, and grant me the courage to say yes loudly and proudly.

Oppressing the Poor

> Oppressing the poor in order to enrich oneself,
>   and giving to the rich, will lead only to loss.
>
>   (Proverbs 22:16)

Most of us don't seek to oppress the poor. We try to help the poor and to be fair and just to those in need. But consider how we might oppress the poor without meaning to. Overconsuming and overindulging oppresses the poor. Hoarding finite resources like clothes or food or money oppresses the poor. Ignoring the homeless who need a place to sleep oppresses the poor. Preventing others from helping oppresses the poor. How can we avoid the offense of oppression, even when we don't set out to ignore others' needs? We can cultivate intention and purpose in everything we do, rather than going through life on autopilot, not thinking about what we're doing. Today, start practicing intentionality by considering your actions. Do they support the poor or needy, or do they make their lot harder, directly or indirectly?

God of justice and love, help me to be intentional in my actions and find ways to help the poor.

Praise for the Year

> Let everything that breathes praise the Lord! Praise the Lord!

> (Psalm 150:6)

Praising God on our own is good. Joining with others in praising God unites us with our fellow human beings. By praising God with all that breathes, we grow in unity with all creation. As we close this calendar year, praising God with all creation puts us on the right path to start another year. Take time on this last day of the year to praise God with others. Together honor all that has happened in your lives, put the past year in perspective, and prepare for the year to come. What praise can we offer God to wrap up this year?

God, thank you for the gift of this past year, with all its ups and downs. Help me to go into next year with praise and thanksgiving, a clean heart, and a renewed commitment to following you.

Index of Themes

Reflections are provided for each of the following themes, which can be located by turning to the corresponding calendar dates.

Acceptance: January 3, January 26, January 27, February 2, March 4, April 3, May 3, June 2, July 2, August 2, September 1, September 5, October 1, October 16, November 3, December 3

Anger: January 16, February 2, February 9, February 16, March 17, April 16, May 16, June 15, July 16, August 15, September 14, October 14, November 16, December 16

Being Christian: January 19, February 19, March 20, April 19, May 19, June 18, July 19, August 18, September 17, October 17, November 13, November 19, November 21, December 19, December 22

Bullying: January 8, February 7, February 25, March 9, March 30, April 8, May 8, June 7, July 8, August 7, September 6, October 6, November 8, December 8

Commitment: January 17, February 17, March 18, April 17, May 17, June 16, July 17, August 16, September 15, October 15, November 17, December 17

Dating: January 12, February 11, March 13, April 12, May 12, June 11, July 12, August 11, September 10, October 10, November 12, December 12

Doubt: January 13, February 12, March 14, April 13, May 13, June 12, July 13, August 12, October 11, December 13

Environment: January 30, March 1, March 31, April 30, May 30, June 29, July 30, August 29, September 28, October 28

Faith and Values: January 11, January 14, February 10, February 12, February 23, March 12, March 19, April 11, May 11, June 10, July 11, August 10, September 9, October 9, November 11, December 11

Fear: January 18, February 8, February 18, March 19, April 18, May 15, May 18, June 17, July 18, August 17, August 22, September 16, October 16, November 18, December 18

Feeling Safe: January 9, February 8, March 10, April 9, May 9, June 8, July 9, August 8, September 7, October 7, October 11, November 9, December 9

Forgiveness: January 20, February 20, March 21, March 23, April 20, May 20, June 19, July 20, August 19, September 5, September 15, September 18, October 5, October 18, November 20, December 20

Friendship: January 4, February 3, February 4, March 5, April 4, May 4, June 3, July 3, August 3, September 2, October 2, November 4, December 4

God / Jesus: January 27, February 12, February 25, February 27, March 28, April 27, May 27, June 26, July 27, August 26, September 25, October 25, November 28, December 28, December 31

Happiness: January 22, February 22, March 23, April 22, May 22, June 21, July 22, August 21, September 20, October 20, November 23

Hope: January 23, January 25, February 23, March 24, April 23, May 23, June 22, July 23, August 22, September 21, October 21, November 24, December 23

Identity: January 1, January 31, March 2, March 7, April 1, May 1, May 31, June 30, July 1, July 31, August 30, September 29, October 29, December 1

Justice: January 29, February 21, February 29, March 30, April 29, May 29, June 28, July 29, August 28, September 27, October 27, November 30, December 21, December 30

Love: January 12, January 24, February 14, February 24, March 25, April 2, April 19, April 24, May 24, June 23, July 24, August 23, September 22, October 22, November 25, December 23, December 24

Money: January 14, February 13, March 15, April 14, May 14, June 13, July 14, August 13, September 12, October 12, November 14, December 14, December 22

Parents / Family: January 6, February 5, February 20, March 7, April 6, May 6, June 5, July 6, August 5, September 4, October 4, November 6, December 6

Peer Pressure: January 5, February 4, February 7, March 6, April 5, May 5, June 4, July 5, August 4, September 3, October 3, November 5, December 5

Popularity: January 26, February 26, March 27, April 26, May 26, June 25, July 26, August 25, September 24, October 24, November 27, December 27

School: January 9, January 15, February 15, March 16, April 15, May 15, June 14, July 15, August 14, September 13, October 13, November 15, December 15

Self-Esteem: January 2, January 27, February 1, March 3, April 2, May 2, June 1, July 1, August 1, August 31, September 30, October 30, December 2

Service: January 21, February 21, March 22, March 29, April 21, May 21, June 20, July 21, August 20, September 19, October 19, November 22, December 21

Sexuality: January 7, February 6, March 8, April 7, May 7, June 6, July 7, August 6, October 5, October 10, November 7, November 12, December 7

Suffering: January 25, February 25, March 26, April 25, May 25, June 24, July 25, August 24, September 23, October 23, November 24, November 26, December 26

Violence: January 10, February 9, March 11, April 10, May 10, June 9, July 10, August 9, September 8, October 8, November 10, December 10

Vocation: January 28, February 28, March 29, April 28, May 28, June 27, July 28, August 27, September 26, October 26, November 29, December 29